CW00677052

HIMALAYA

HIMALAYA

GANESH SAILI

**TIGER BOOKS
INTERNATIONAL
LONDON**

All rights reserved. No part of this publication may be transmitted or reproduced in any form or by any means without prior permission of the publisher.

To Abha—Ganesh Saili

ISBN: 1-85501-849-7

This edition published in 1996 by **Tiger Books International PLC,** Twickenham

© **Lustre Press Pvt. Ltd., 1996**
M - 75, G K - II Market, New Delhi - 110 048, INDIA
Tel.: (011) 6442271, 6462782, 6460886-0887
Fax: (011) 6467185

Conceived and designed by
Pramod Kapoor at Roli CAD Centre

Text editor:
Bela Butalia

Production Coordinator:
Naresh Nigam

Typesetting:
Naresh L. Mondal

Photographs:
B.P.S. Walia
Ganesh Saili
Joanna Van Gruisen
Mani Lama
Capt. M.S. Kohli
Pramod Kapoor
Ramesh Pathania
R.K. Gaur
Sanjay Acharya
Sanjeev Saith
Serbjeet Singh

From Fotomedia:
Anita Prasher
Hashmat Singh
Rahul Sharma
R.S. Chundawat
Sanjay Saxena
Shama Ketkar
Sujoy Das

Printed and bound at Star Standard Industries Pte. Ltd., Singapore

CONTENTS

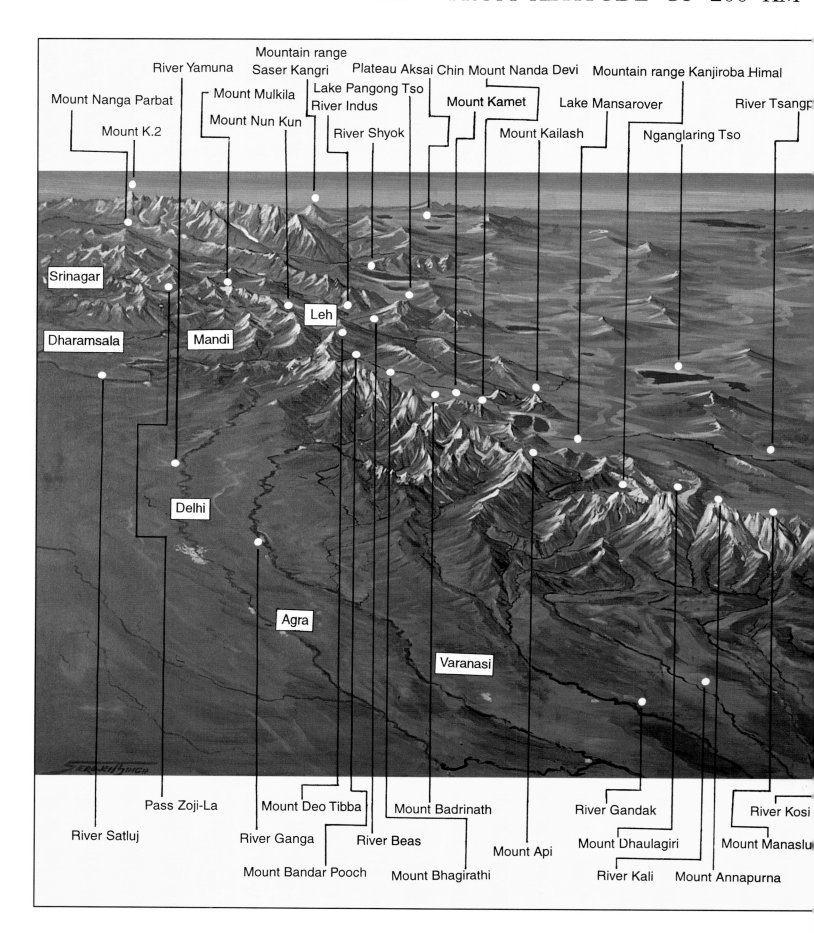

Mountain range
River Yamuna   Saser Kangri   Plateau Aksai Chin Mount Nanda Devi   Mountain range Kanjiroba Himal
Mount Nanga Parbat   Mount Mulkila   Lake Pangong Tso   Mount Kamet   Lake Mansarover   River Tsangp
Mount K.2   Mount Nun Kun   River Indus   Mount Kailash   Nganglaring Tso
River Shyok

Srinagar

Leh

Dharamsala   Mandi

Delhi

Agra

Varanasi

Pass Zoji-La   Mount Deo Tibba   Mount Badrinath   River Gandak   River Kosi

River Satluj   River Ganga   River Beas   Mount Api   Mount Dhaulagiri   Mount Manaslu

Mount Bandar Pooch   Mount Bhagirathi   River Kali   Mount Annapurna

Great PANORAMA
ABOVE PATNA LOOKING NORTH

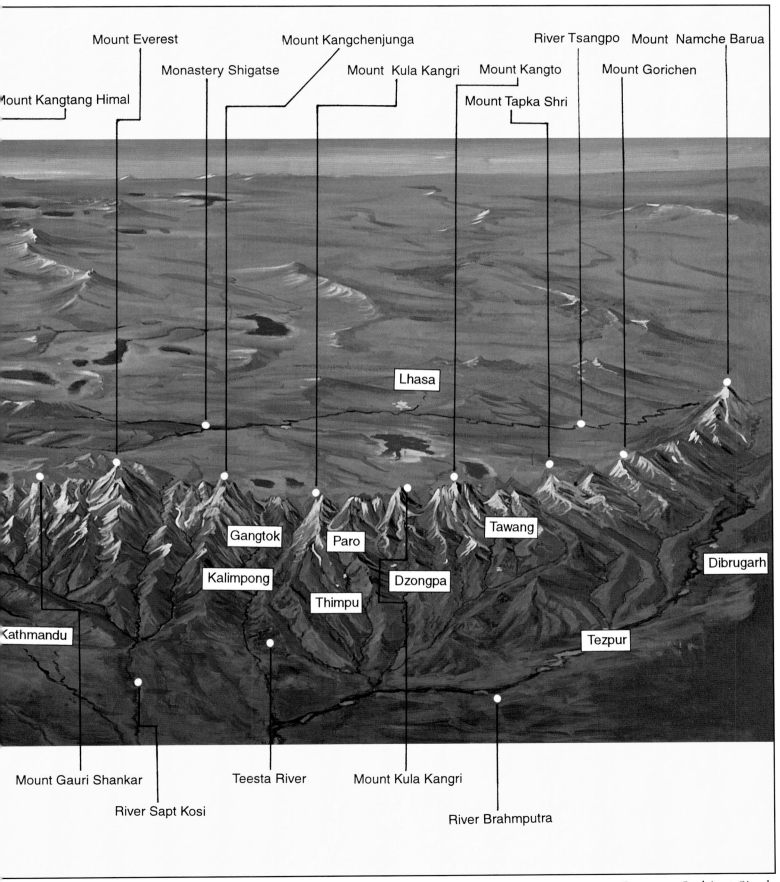

Mount Everest

Mount Kangchenjunga

Monastery Shigatse

Mount Kula Kangri

Mount Kangto

River Tsangpo

Mount Namche Barua

Mount Gorichen

Mount Tapka Shri

Mount Kangtang Himal

Lhasa

Gangtok

Paro

Tawang

Dibrugarh

Kalimpong

Dzongpa

Thimpu

Kathmandu

Tezpur

Mount Gauri Shankar

Teesta River

Mount Kula Kangri

River Sapt Kosi

River Brahmputra

Courtesy: Serbjeet Singh

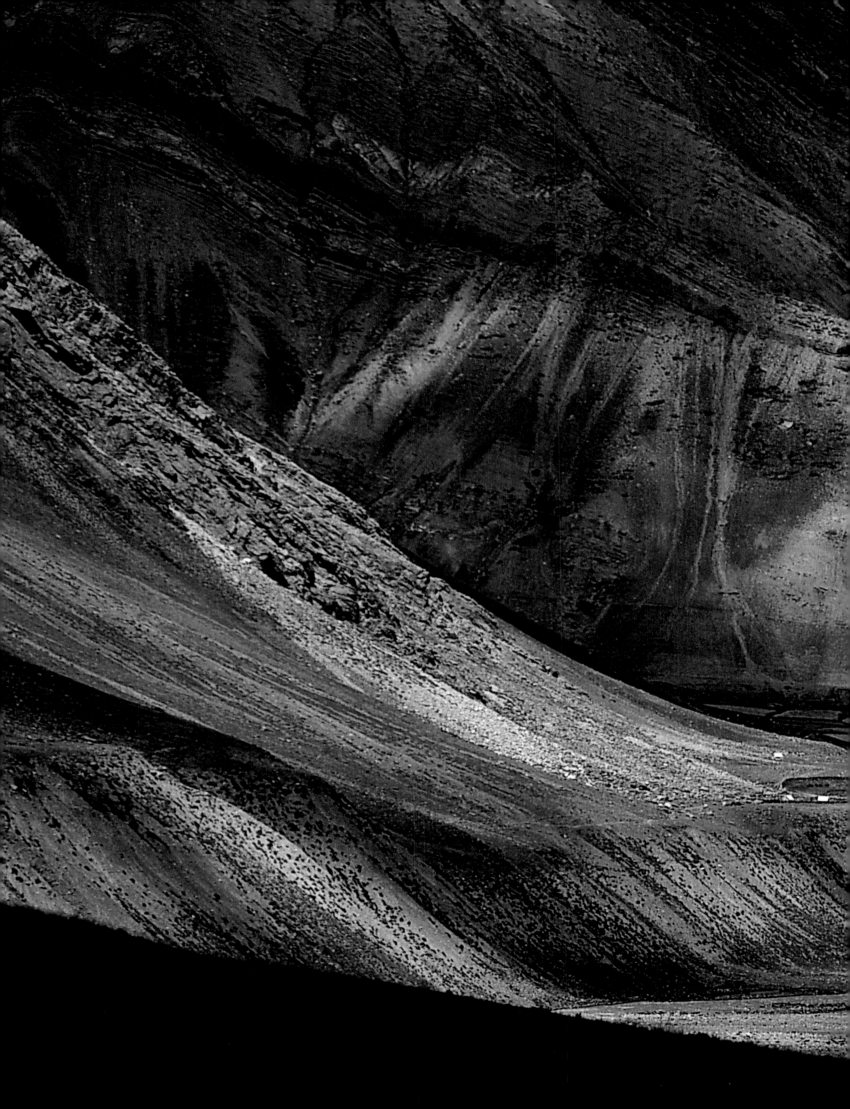

Preceding pages 2-3: Sunrise on Mt. Chomolhari at 23,997 ft in Bhutan.
Pages 4-5: Mishimis tribals of Arunachal Pradesh.
Pages 8-9 Likir monastery, Ladakh, belongs to the Gelugpa (Yellow Hats) sect of Buddhism. The sect preaches a return to the original form of Buddhism, free from tantric and magical influences.
Pages 10-11: Pin Valley, Spiti, in Himachal Pradesh.
Following pages 14-15: Festival at Thikse monastery, Ladakh.
Pages 16-17: Shivling Peak (6,544 m).

A gigantic Bhairub image worshipped during Indra Jatra in Nepal.

13

INTRODUCTION

The Himalayas—or if one prefers, *the* Himalayas, the Abode of Snow—are the most stupendous mountain ranges on the entire face of the earth. They seem to invite superlatives for they *are* the ultimate superlative. Where else would one go looking for the highest peak, the highest pass, the highest surviving plant or the rarest surviving animal? All other things dwarf in comparison to what has been aptly called the greatest physical feature of the earth.

This much and more is all encompassed in a wide sweeping arc that curves like a swathe some 2,400 kilometres long, if measured from the Pamirs west of a bend in the river Indus, and stretches all the way to the river Brahmputra in eastern Assam. If you look to the north, it is 300 kilometres wide and rises over eight kilometres above mean sea-level.

'In a hundred ages of the gods, I could not tell you of the glories of the Himalayas', sang the ancient poet of the Skanda Purana and in doing so, came closer than anyone else to the truth. For these mountains continue to defy the written word. The sea has had writers like Stevenson and Conrad, Melville and Hemingway. We have climbed the celestial peaks of the Himalayas and crossed remote passes, but still they have kept their secrecy and reserve, remaining aloof, mysterious and forbidding. Since the dawn of time, men have looked up at them with a strange mixture of awe and reverence, a feeling echoed in the words of Nehru: 'They have always been a part of our history and tradition, our thinking and our poetry, our worship and our devotion . . . according to our mythology, they are the abode of the gods.'

While other mountain ranges remain a part of the landscape, slashed across the face of the earth, with roads and even trains chugging through them, none has yet willed a rail-line across the Himalayas and in most places there are no roads to lead you on to where only a few intrepid souls have dared to go. True, you can now fly over these mountains but you cannot burrow through them; furtively climb them but never really subdue them; they remain unbeatable—the ultimate frontier.

How did they come to be there? This is a question best left to geologists. It all began, we are told, at the beginning when the earth was wrapped in primordial mist. Time was unborn and Man was to await his turn on the timeless shores of Lethe as two great land masses moved towards each other through a rapidly receding sea. The epic collision gave birth to the unique Himalayas.

Down the ages, these mountains have been venerated, feared and worshipped by those who have lived in their proximity. It was once believed that the climbing of the peaks would invite the wrath of the gods who dwelt there. In the pioneering days of mountain climbing, permission to climb some of these misty peaks was given with the rider that the actual summit would not be defiled. A British expedition to the Kangchenjunga in 1955 kept its word and stopped twenty feet away from the main cone. Similarly, another one to Machapuchare halted 150 feet from the summit, in deference, so to speak, to the belief that the summit was only for the gods.

It is easy to understand why the peaks have such charming names: Annapurna, the Giver of Life; Chomolungma, Goddess Mother of the Earth, the Tibetan name for the Everest group; Dhaulagiri, the White Mountain; Nanga Parbat, the Naked Mountain; Bandar Poonch, the Monkey's Tail; Mrigthuni, the Deer's Chin, and Machapuchare, the Fish Tail.

Even glaciers like the Siachen have a name: the Great Rose. This longest of glaciers in the world borrows its fine name from the wild roses thriving near its snout. On the other hand, the Sia Kangri is the Ice Mountain of the Rose, named thus after the glacier below it.

Other names evoke lesser known legends: Kampire Dior is the Home of the Old Hag; Boiohaghur Duanasir is Where Only the Devil's Horse Can Go and in Chitral is Tirich Mir, which is reportedly guarded by giant frogs, only too ready to pounce on anyone daring to

Facing page: Mt. Machapuchare (6,993 m), or the Fish Tail, in Nepal.

19

come near it. A Norwegian team which reached the summit of Tirich Mir was wonderstruck. 'From where we stood,' wrote an ecstatic H.R.A. Streather, 'with a turn of the head, we could look into Pakistan, Afghanistan, Russia, China, Kashmir and possibly even Tibet.'

Could one ask for more?

Or take the grandeur of the Central Himalayas, the spectacular views and the sheer splendour of the Garhwal-Kumaon ranges. Foremost among these visual stunners is the island sanctuary of Nanda Devi.

'She imposes upon her votaries an admission test beyond their skill and endurance,' wrote the explorer H.W. Tilman as he set out with Eric Shipton to find a route to the elusive peak, 'a seventy-mile barrier-ring on which stand twelve measured peaks over 21,000 feet high, and which has no depression lower than 17,000 feet, except in the west where the Rishi Ganga, rising at the foot of Nanda Devi and draining an area of 250 square miles of ice and snow, has carved for itself what must be one of the most terrific gorges in the world.'

Two internal ridges, converging upon this river from the north and south, form, as it were, the curtains of an inner sanctuary, within which the great mountain soars up to 25,660 feet. Nanda Devi is like a queen surrounded by courtiers, worshipped by the gentle mountain folk as they sing poems of praise to the Mother Goddess:

'Victory to Nanda, Amba and Jagtamba!
Victory to Nanda and Jagtamba Bhawani!
Victory to the Great Goddess, Bearer of the Parasol!
May success come to the Daughter of the Gods!'

Songs like these echo in the hills as pilgrims wind their way through the high mountains to the lost lake of Roopkund, which continues to keep its icy secrets hidden from mortal view.

Just one such view is from Binsar, a 300 kilometre sweep that takes the breath away—

Facing page: Nanda Devi (7,818 m), the supreme goddess of the Garhwal Himalayas, is the highest mountain in India. It is surrounded by 12 measured peaks, each over 6,300 m high.

from Gangotri in Garhwal to the borders of Nepal. Trishul (the Trident) shoulders the ranges up to Nanda Devi; then comes the conical dome of Nanda Ghunti offset by the citadel of Chaukhamba; nearby are the cathedral spires of Nilkanth, the Blue-Throated One and Kamet. Panch Chuli or the Cooking Stalls of the Gods lies to the east.

Rising from the great plains of northern India and the Tibetan plateau are three major mountain zones. First are the Siwaliks (the Eyebrows of Shiva), long, narrow and low, stretching from the Punjab to Assam. They run parallel to the base of the Himalayas from the river Indus to the Brahmputra river over a distance of 1,500 miles. Between the two are dense forests, home to tigers, panthers, bears and various other wild animals.

The Lesser Himalayas are a fragile zone bearing the brunt of the torrential powers of the monsoon. They are about sixty miles wide. Vast coniferous forests form a canopy over the lower regions where during the Raj the British found time to get away from the heat and dust, in the more salubrious climes of the hill-stations of Dalhousie, Simla, Mussoorie, Ranikhet, Almora, Nainital and Darjeeling. The highest peaks in the Inner Himalayas are around 15,000 feet.

The Greater Himalayas have peaks which are seldom below 18,000 feet. In this abode of ice are 31 peaks over 25,000 feet of which a dozen are over 26,000 feet. Abutting the Tibetan highlands to the north, these are the highest features on the face of the earth.

At the western edge of these highlands are the rugged lands of Ladakh, Zanskar and the Karakoram mountains where at 28,250 feet, K-2 is the second highest mountain with 18 other peaks over 25,000 feet. Frank Smythe captured in words some of their enigma and mysticism when he said:

We saw that we had entered the Kingdom of Flowers. Bareness was replaced by beauty . . . As we descended, the flora became more luscious, until we were wading knee-deep through an ocean of flowers, ranging in colour from the sky blue of the poppies to the deep wine red of the potentillas . . . It is a place of escape for those wearied of modern civilization.

Chapter 1

KARAKORAMS

Down the ages men have crossed the mountains for different reasons. Some did so for reasons of commerce; others in search of the Gods strode across on pilgrimages, while the old scourge of war egged on a few hardy souls. One of the earliest to do so was Hannibal. Astride his elephants he crossed the Alps in 218 BC, surprising everybody, including himself. Two thousand years after this great feat did man get to the summit of Mont Blanc. In 1787, de Saussure, a scientist from Geneva, went to the mountain accompanied by no less than eighteen guides who were carrying every contraption possible. Far, far away from the Alps, in the east were the Hindu Kush mountains. The Greeks called them the Paropanisos—'higher than the eagle's flight'. A major chunk of this range lies in Afghanistan. The part that lies in Pakistan is called the Chitral. It is a place which takes the breath away. Four of its major peaks are over 7,000 metres high. Still sheltered from the civilizing influences of the modern world, it was through the 11,600 feet Khowak Pass in Chitral that Alexander the Great came with his army in the dead of winter, much to the chagrin of his enemies. It was a route others were to follow down the ages.

One of the mightiest mountain ranges in the world are the Karakorams, which seem to brush aside man's puny measures in a single sweep. These rugged natural fortresses divide the Kashmir Himalayas from China, running some 300 miles from the Afghan border to the Shyok river, almost parallel to the Punjab Himalayas, with the valley of the Indus in between.

The green-blue waters of the Indus lend a touch of colour to the desiccated mountains as they make their 1,800 mile journey to the Arabian Sea. Gigantic boulders try to stem the river's entrapped waters. But water always triumphs. 'Be like water,' advises Tao Tse Ching 'if it cannot go over, it goes under.' But water always wins and nowhere else is this so fully illustrated as in the confining gorges of the Karakorams.

One has to see the Indus at work to fully comprehend the power of a gushing river as it chisels its way through what to any other force would be insurmountable barriers. Rising at the foot of Mount Kailash, venerated by Hindus and Buddhists, it flows on, unruffled, with a single-mindedness, unaided by the rain, for the clouds, that are such a help to other rivers elsewhere, simply never reach this far. Small wonder then that the Indus lends its name to a great civilization that has lasted a thousand years.

Land of Light

In the bleak world of the Karakoram ranges, the villages remain tiny oases against a backdrop of stony ridges. In their calcinated, terraced fields are orchards watered by glacier-fed streams.

Hunza is one such place. According to legend, the local population are the descendants of soldiers who stayed behind as Alexander marched into the plains of India. Be it fact or fiction, the inhabitants are fair, blue-eyed and blonde.

Up until 1889, the area was a part of the state of Jammu and Kashmir. Gilgit lay along the ancient Silk Route of caravans travelling from ancient India to Central Asia. To put an end to the tradition of pillage and plunder, a campaign was mounted in 1891-92 in which a group led by Lieutenant Manners-Smith showed exceptional bravery by ascending a 1,200-foot cliff to capture the fort at Nilt. He was awarded the Victoria Cross.

There was another route to Gilgit via the Burzil Pass in Kashmir—taking two weeks of

Facing page: The sacred Mt. Kailash (6,740 m), north face, in Tibet. The Hindus have worshipped it as the abode of Shiva and his consort Parvati since times immemorial. The route to Mt. Kailash is even prescribed in the Hindu scriptures.

travel by road. Yet this is all part of the vanished past. In the spring of 1929, four planes of the Royal Air Force flew along the gorge of the Indus and landed in Gilgit. Stunned by the 'monsters' from the sky in their midst, the inhabitants are reported to have brought bales of hay to 'satiate their voracious appetite'!

Today, it is all of an hour's flight from Rawalpindi.

Along these ranges lie a trail of memories:

characters of Ariosto or Tasso seem destined to appear in the most natural manners.' It was in these words that in 1959 the Orientalist, Fosco Maraini, who had just come back from a gruelling expedition to Saraghrar peak, described his arrival in the Kafir Valleys.

Spread over an area of some 5,000 square miles is the land which was known in early times as 'the land of the unbelievers' or *kafirs*. In each one of its three riverine valleys dwells a tribe distinct from the others. While the *Siah*

View from Sera, southwest Tibet, on the way to Mt. Kailash from Humla.

Buddhism took the route along these ranges to Ladakh and Tibet; Huien Tsang trudged from China to India in fourteen years and Babur in his *Memoirs* remembers a blizzard as his army almost got lost while making its way through Zirrin Pass on an expedition from Khorasam to Kabul.

Nuristan is a place of romance, hedged in by formidable mountains on all sides: the Hindu Kush ranges, the Indus river and the deserts of Central Asia to the north; the Bagshul range to the northeast; the Kunar river to the southeast where it meets the Kabul river; and the mountains which rise above the banks of the Kabul river to the west.

'Suddenly, the trail seemed to disappear into a forest of willows, mulberries and other trees. It was one of those valleys where the

Posh or the black-robed ones get their name from their black robes, the *Safed-Posh* wear white robes. They speaks in different tongues hard for an outsider to comprehend.

In the 13th century, Genghis Khan was to meet them and in the following century Timur Leng was to fight them. In 1602, during the reign of the Moghuls, a Portuguese Jesuit was to travel from Lahore to China as part of a merchant caravan. He wrote of a place in the eastern Hindu Kush where grapes grew aplenty and the wine was excellent. Two centuries of silence followed till Alexander Gardner made two journeys through Kafiristan and lived to tell the tale.

The Scottish author George Robertson was to describe it thus in 1896: 'The class that holds power is made up of descendants of the

Bactrian colonists who must have had a great deal of Greek blood in their veins. Because of their refusal to bow to Islam, in the ninth and tenth centuries, they were forced to abandon the more fertile lowlands and to seek shelter up here in the mountains.' Recent studies describe the Kafir as a people of Indo-Aryan descent, speaking a language akin to Sanskrit, worshipping a pantheon similar to that of the Vedic gods and the deities of Turkestan. Yet their European and Asiatic roots were of no great help in the slaughter they were subjected to.

In 1895, under the protection of the Durand Line which marked the end of British influence over these mountains, the Afghan Emir, Abdur Rahman Khan, took to the sword. Idols vanished, mosques sprouted and Kafiristan changed its very name to Nuristan, the 'land of light'.

The Great Game, as it was known, between Russia and Britain started in the last decades of the 19th century. Disguised surveyors began to make clandestine trips to the forbidden lands. One such man was a certain W. W. Macnair, an officer of the Survey of India, who, disguising himself as a *hakim*, entered the Bashgul valley to find its legendary inhabitants with Caucasian complexions living a life of idyllic bliss.

A crystal clear picture emerged when the British Political Agent in Gilgit spent two years (1890 to 1891) writing a comprehensive book *The Kafirs of the Hindu Kush*. Just as well, for even as he was putting his pen to paper, tribes were converting to Islam and the old pagan ways—full of mystery and remoteness—were vanishing forever.

This pastoral paradise was torn asunder in 1895 by Abdur Rahman Khan. He had had enough of the weird ways of the hill-tribes. There was also the possibility that one day the Russians might simply annex the land. Troops under the command of Ghulam Hyder Khan launched a three-pronged attack against the land of the Kafirs. Hundreds of hill folk perished as village after village was put to torch, though valiantly defended by primitive bows and arrows.

When the dust settled, phoenix-like from the ashes of war rose Nuristan—the Land of Light.

Nanga Parbat Peak

Of the numerous peaks in this region, Nanga Parbat Peak has passed into mountaineering lexicon. It stands remote and aloof, at the western edge of these ranges. Its name, the Naked Mountain, describes the peak better than anything else: its sharp ridges can hold little snow and this unclad appearance is most unusual in zones where all its peers are modestly wrapped in a white mantle of snow. It is much favoured by most climbers, more so the Germans, who have given it the epithet, Murder Mountain.

The explorer, Albert Frederick Mummery, was the first to venture on this mountain. His was an audacious attempt. Leaving London on June 20, 1895, he caught a ship at Brindisi for Bombay, changed to another for Rawalpindi, arriving there on 17 July.

Three days later, he was within sight of Nanga Parbat. He camped at the base of the remarkable Rupal Face. It is one of the most spectacular, dangerous and difficult of inclines in the world. Mummery crossed the 5,505 metres Diamir Col, reached Diamir Peak at 5,800 metres and carried on to an altitude of 6,400 metres, over an unnamed peak of some 6,500 metres.

On August 20, he set out to make an attempt to ascend the peak up the Diamir Face. He had already set up two camps, one at 4,580 metres and one at 5,100 metres. Four days later, the three climbers were seen climbing the upper slopes of the glacier. That was the last that was heard of them.

Daunting and wild, bearing the onslaught of gnawing wind and torrential rain during the monsoons, Nanga Parbat is full of the dangers of the unknown. The Sherpas call it the man-eater or the 'Mountain of the Devil'. Maybe they are right. No other peak has claimed lives with such sickening regularity. The list of tragedies is heart-breaking. In 1934, a German expedition under Willi Merkl managed to reach an altitude of 7,800 metres before a blizzard killed four climbers and six Sherpas. Just three years later, a rampaging avalanche at Camp IV buried all the seven climbers and nine high-altitude Sherpas of yet another expedition.

The peak fell on July 3, 1953 to the

Austrian, Herman Buhl. Aged 29, he climbed solo over the last 1,300 metres of Rakhiot Face to the top. In 1961, Low and two other climbers found success via the Diamir Face, but Low lost his life while descending.

On June 27, 1970, Karl Herigkoffer and the brothers Reinold and Gunther Messner climbed the summit. Exhausted, without food, tents or rope, they came down the mountain. It was three days of an inordinately tough ordeal. Gunther was

Starting off with a guide, eight camels, a servant and an assistant, the first stage went rather well. For the first thousand miles traversed he met no other human. Another forty days march to Kashgar in Turkestan before turning south to Yarkand—then he saw the towering mountains . . .

From here he could well have taken the easier route to Leh, the capital of Ladakh, but he chose the lesser road through Mustagh Pass and into Kashmir. At this point, his guide,

Karakoram Range, seen from Nubra Valley, Ladakh.

killed in an avalanche. Reinold survived, but with massive frostbites.

'A pillar of rock and ice,' wrote Matthias Rebitsch, a fine mountaineer of his times, of the Rupal Face of Nanga Parbat in 1938, 'of almost otherworldly size. To us it was a quintessentially impossible dream.' And Nanga Parbat continues to entrap in its icy embrace those who go out to conquer her.

Lower down, the valley of Hunza is most favoured by travellers. The rest is inhospitable, especially towards the east where the peaks scrape the sky. The travels of Francis Younghusband made him the first European to set foot here. Starting from Peking in 1887, he decided he would get to India through the Gobi Desert and the Karakorams—three thousand miles of territory unknown to man.

Wali, accompanied by seven other men and ponies, lost his way. Cresting the 15,000 feet pass, they saw a view they would never forget: row upon row of mountains stood before them.

'It was a scene, which—as I viewed it, and realized that this seemingly impregnable array must be pierced and overcome—seemed to put iron into my soul.' Descending lower, there was more to come.

I chanced to look upwards rather suddenly, and a sight met my eyes which fairly staggered me. We had just turned a corner which brought into view a peak of appalling height, which could be no other than K 2. Viewed from this direction, it seemed to rise in an almost perfect cone, but to an inconceivable height. We were quite close under it, and here on the northern side where it is literally clothed in glacier, there must have been 14,000 to 16,000 feet of solid ice.

More was to come. On reaching the top of the 19,030 feet high Mustagh Pass, they looked down upon a vista that would send a chill up their spines—quite literally too.

A precipice yawned at them.

as I gave no order to go back, I meant to go on.

Without much ado they started sliding down the icy slope. Younghusband wrapped handkerchiefs around his boots for a bit of extra grip. Wali cut steps with an ice-axe. Arriving at the edge of an abyss, they looked down.

It took six hours of scrambling down a rock face to reach the bottom. Glancing backwards,

Mt. Mutagata (7,546 m) viewed from far southwest China, near Pakistan.

To get down seemed to me an impossibility. I had no experience of Alpine climbing, and had no ice-axe. I had not even proper boots. All I had for footwear were some native boots of soft leather without nails and without heels . . . which gave me no sort of grip on any icy surface. I kept quite silent as I looked over the pass, and waited to hear what the men had to say about it. They meanwhile were looking at me, and imagining that an Englishman never went back from an enterprise he had once started, took it as a matter of course that

he said: 'It seemed impossible that any man could have come down such a place.'

Walking on for several days through Skardu in Baltistan they arrived in Srinagar, Kashmir. Seven months had passed since they set out from China and the first Englishman who greeted Younghusband merely said: 'Don't you think you should have a wash?'

In the last century, roads have been built in the Karakorams but little else has changed. While men and their matters perish, the Karakorams are forever.

Chapter 2

KASHMIR AND HIMACHAL

The Great Himalayan crest-zone takes a turn southeast from the massif of Nanga Parbat to the twin Nun Kun peaks and then goes on towards the Himachal Himalayas. Nowhere do the ranges go over 20,000 feet and they only begin to climb after they are well into the neighbouring zone.

The Pir Panjal ranges form a serrated rim towards the south, dividing the vale of Kashmir from Jammu, while the Dhauladar and Siwaliks form a margin around Jammu. It is a land of water: the Chenab rises in Himachal as the Chandra and Bhaga, crossing the line near Kilar before going on to Kishtwar. Crossing the Chenab, the traveller goes through a tunnel in the Pir Panjal and then along a road on the banks of the Jhelum to Anantnag and Srinagar.

KASHMIR

Fabled Kashmir, a paradise on earth. Where shimmering lakes merge with snow-capped mountains to stun the senses. A new vista greets the traveller at every little curve on the road.

Francois Bernier accompanied the entourage of the Moghul Emperor to the vale of Kashmir in 1664 and gave us a graphic account of his travels in *Journey to Kachemire—The Paradise of the Indies*. On the twelfth of March, they had been on the road from Lahore for twelve long days. The remains of that Sarai where they encamped are still there in the town of Bhimbhar, a large building about 300 square feet, where the emperor and his personal attendants used to stay. It must have been a relief to leave these suffocating quarters and get on to the goal ahead. Only a select few were allowed in the valley, lest the influx of a largish group produce a scarcity of provisions in the small kingdom. An eagle-eyed Omrah stood at

Facing page: Festival at the Tabo Gompa (c. 996), Spiti, one of the oldest monasteries in the country with the head lama conducting the rites. Tabo monastery celebrated its millennium in June 1996.
Following pages 30-31: *Sopore on the Jhelum, Kashmir.*

the entrance to the pass: all those not permitted would not get to see the diamond air of this heaven on Earth.

The king, of course, took a few of his choicest elephants for the baggage and the women of his seraglio. 'Though heavy footed and unwieldy, these animals are yet very sure-footed, feeling their way when the road is difficult and dangerous, and assuring themselves of the firm hold of one foot before they move another.' True words these, but a tragedy did occur later in the trip. That's another story.

The French narrator delighted in what he saw. The first mountains nearest to the plains were of moderate height, of the freshest verdure, decked with trees and covered with pastureland. An abundance of wildlife. Beyond these mountains rose others of greater altitude, whose summits, at all times, were covered with snow, soaring above the clouds and mist and 'like Mount Olympus, are constantly bright and serene'.

It was the abundance of water which surprised him. Water gushed from innumerable springs, irrigating the fields through little channels going to the furthest hillock. These waters, separated into a thousand rivulets, produced a thousand cascades before collecting to form the Jhelum, which wended its way through the kingdom, passing through Srinagar before taking a turn at Baramulla, flowing through a gorge to fall into the Chenab.

It was a place of gardens. Most houses along the banks of the river had little gardens, 'which produce a very pretty effect, especially in the spring and summer . . . Indeed most houses in the city also have their gardens; and many have a canal, on which the owner keeps a pleasure-boat, thus communicating with the lake.'

Three centuries later, the gardens are still the same. It is raining across the Dal Lake at the end of May. Little can be seen except heavy mist and lowering clouds. You put on a cap and raincoat or take a brolly and start off for a walk over the bridge at Dal Gate towards the town. Surely the rain must have washed out the drains

which had long been untouched. Every now and then you have to grasp your nostrils firmly with a handkerchief only to take it away again as a fragrant scent is borne to you from some bush of jasmine, or an old wall covered with roses.

The town seems a strange mixture of squalor and loveliness. There are old wooden houses of quaint design, two or three storeys high, with overhanging balconies and richly carved brackets. The sloping roofs are covered with

reward. For, nice to say, the morrow *was* a lovely day.

The first visible sign of rejoicing is the appearance, in the houseboats, of washed sheets, blankets and bright-hued quilts, all hung upon the roof-tops to dry. The Dal Lake, a ten square-mile sheet of water, is so clear that every passing shadow seems mirrored in it.

Who has not heard of the gardens of Kashmir created by the Moghul gardeners, who were poets, weaving their lovely effects out of trees

Gurez Valley, Kashmir.

earth upon which grass and flowers grow. In the by-streets and tortuous lanes the houses are a huddle of tenements. Concerning the sanitation one dare not even make conjectures. It must be that long ago some great benefactor smelt the unpleasant odours of the town's gutters and scattered the seeds of all sweet-scented trees, plants and flowers. Roses and jasmine flourish everywhere, filling the air with a perfume which lingers for long.

The first person you encounter on your return from your walk is an optimist who emphatically announces: 'Tomorrow will be a lovely day.' In olden times, soothsayers were often richly rewarded. Joseph was made a great man in Egypt for predicting a famine. So it is hoped that this old gentleman who promises beautiful weather will one day reap an adequate

and flowers, water and sky? The Chasma Shai, or 'King's Fountain' is a small garden, lying at the foot of the hills near Parimahal. It has prettily laid-out flower-beds, and its great chinars are so old and beautiful that one must pass them with the reverence due to centenarians. In the center of the garden is a watercourse bordered by stone parapets with waterfalls leaping in cascades from terrace to terrace. These terraces and waterfalls are a common feature of all the Moghul gardens in Kashmir.

If you wander through the Nishat Bagh, 'The Garden of the Morning Wind', you will find great leafy chinars, deodars, dark firs, and sheets of brilliant flowers. The pansies, like carpets of purple or golden velvet, the zinnias, godetias and balsams were bunched in patches of scarlet and orange, rose and heliotrope. There is again the poetic conception of a garden whose chief attraction lies in the play of water.

Looking back on the memories of that time, it is hard to say today what gives you the greatest delight, your wayfaring, or the beauty awaiting you at each destination. It was a joy merely to travel along the roads and feast your eyes on the vista of blue sky and snowclad mountains. And the trees were gracious company. Francois Bernier was a highly educated French doctor with a roving eye and a special talent for scandalmongering. He narrates:

> The people of Kachemire are proverbial for their clear complexions and fine forms. The women especially are very handsome; and it is from this country that nearly every individual, when first admitted to the court of the Great Moghul, selects wives or concubines, that his children may be whiter than the Indians and pass for genuine Moghuls. Unquestionably there must be beautiful women among the higher classes if we may judge by those of the orders seen in the streets and in the shops.

In those days, as well as today, women as well as men were seen to wear shawls around their heads or to pass them over the left shoulder as a mantle. There are two kinds made today: one kind with the wool of the country, fine and delicate; the other kind with the wool, or rather hair, of the wild antelopes wandering in the upper reaches of the high mountains, called *touz*.

So prized were these find shawls that by Article X of the Treaty of March 16, 1846, by which the British made over in perpetuity, as an independent possession, the Kashmir region to Maharaja Gulab Singh of Jammu, the latter bound himself and his heirs for ever to acknowledge the supremacy of the British. In token, he promised to present every year to them, 'one horse, twelve prefect shawl goats of approved breed (six males and six females) and three pairs of Cashmere shawls'.

How did the Pir Panjal Pass, 11,400 feet above sea-level, get its name? It could have been named after the *fakir* who was buried at the top of the pass, and whose shrine is a place of worship even in present times. In Persian, *pir* means a saint. *Pirs* have been known to

establish themselves in way out places for meditating on the works of the Creator. Panjal is the name of the high range close by. A rough translation of Pir Panjal can well be translated as the Pass of the Great Range.

On the edge of Nagin lake is the place where the Mirzai sect of Muslims believe is the grave of Jesus. It is said Jesus did not die on the Cross but travelled here to live and spread the message of peace and to pass away at the ripe old age of 136 years.

For long, there has been the persistent belief that the original settlers in the valley were a tribe from Israel, who moved here after the great exodus from the land of Egypt, with Moses in the lead. So strident were these tales that Bernier was constrained to refer to them. He found no trace of the Jews for the entire population was 'either Gentile or Mahometan'.

And yet wheresoever he went he saw signs of Judaism. The inhabitants of the frontier villages of the Pir Panjal struck him as resembling the Jews. Their countenance and manner and the singular peculiarity which makes it possible for a traveller to identify the inhabitants of one country with another, all point to their Jewish descent. 'You are not to ascribe what I say to mere fancy,' remarks the proud Bernier, 'the Jewish appearance of these villagers having been remarked by our Jesuit Father, and by several other Europeans, long before I visited Kachemire.'

Then there is the prevalence of the name Mousa, which is no other than Moses, in a city where most of the inhabitants are Muslims. Another common tradition has it that Solomon the Wise came to this countryside and opened a passage for the waters by cutting into the mountain at Baramulla. It is believed that the Throne of Solomon, the ancient edifice on one of the nearby hills, was built by Solomon.

But it was not always so. There was a blend of diverse cultures where the call of the *muezzin* mingled with the fragrance of the joss-sticks from the Buddhist monasteries and the tinkle of bells of the Raghunath Temple.

Tucked away in the high mountains is the holy shrine of Amarnath at 16,000 feet to which flock pilgrims, the young and the aged, the weak and the infirm, all on their way to see the waxing and waning of a *lingam* of ice.

The paradisical alpine meadows of Gulmarg

are always a treat. This is, quite literally, a meadow of flowers when its not too busy being the world's highest golf course or a place for skiing.

Pahalgam lies along the banks of the Lidder river, an angler's dream come true, full of trout brought by the British in the last century.

In autumn, the chinar trees catch fire as the valley takes on russet shades and the leaves hurtle down to the ground. Anyone who has seen Kashmir in autumn will sigh like Nehru: 'It

place. It is unlike any other on the whole of the earth: lost, remote and forbidding.

At Sonamarg, two hours out of Srinagar, is a bridge thrown across the river Sind. The real climb to the famed Zoji-La Pass begins here. At 3,450 metres, the pass, closed in the winter, bears tribute to the perennial courage of our road builders.

Zoji-La is not just a gap in the mountains of the Greater Himalays. It is more of a benchmark, a dividing line, as-it-were, between

Polo game in progress, in Leh, Ladakh, with the monastery perched on the hill-top.

whispers its fairy magic to the ears, and its memory disturbs the mind. How can they who have fallen under its spell release themselves from this enchantment?'

LADAKH: THE BARREN WILDERNESS

Why take the flight to Leh when the best way of getting there is to take the road from Srinagar? If you insist, you may fly there, but the road is better. By road you get a real feel of this remote frontier, at this, the heart of the very crossroads of the high mountains.

A relaxed pace helps the senses to absorb, the body to adjust and the mind to bear up to the rarefied atmosphere ahead. Take it easy and acclimatize yourself rather than haring around the moment you get there. Get used to the

the green vale of Kashmir and the barren crags of a moonscape; between Kashmiri culture and Ladakhi; the picture-postcard perfectness of the former and the handsome ruggedness of the latter. As you cross over to reach the first village on the other side, the mountainfolk retain an *ambiance* not very unlike the Kashmiris, for Dras has the singular distinction of being the coldest place to live in, at least in India.

Kargil is a strange place. A village trying to become a town but never quite making it. In its narrow lanes one is prone to get stuck in traffic jams as the main highway squeezes through its bazaar where the houses seem to huddle together as if for comfort. One has the distinct feeling of being poured, ever so slowly, through a funnel. Understandably, the residents prefer to keep their reserve and not say a word.

This is one place where there is no Eastern charade, you are an intruder and made to feel like one.

Three colours—blue, brown and green—begin to dominate. The sky, the earth and the fields along the river merge into one. Unlike anything one has seen before or will see again. At Namika-La Pass, literally Pillar of the Sky, pinnacles of rock shoulder the sky. The road drops to Bodh Kharbu where, of greater interest is the adjoining area known as Shagkar-Chigtan.

stands for water, and a spire for fire. The stupa is topped with a crescent for air and a solar disc for space. Larger stupas sometimes enclose a room decorated with *mandalas* and iconographic paintings.

En route, the villages blur into a series of zig-zags yet their exotic names remain lodged in memory: Khaltee, Saspol, Basgo, Nyemo and Zanskar will all come back one day like will'o the wisps. Zanskar, the last of these, is a story to wait for at the very end.

Thikse Monastery, 20 km from Leh. The 10 temples of this 12-storey red monastery appear like a fortified construction, and were built sometime in the 15th century. It has 60 resident lamas, and (allegedly) a nunnery.

In the quaint village of Lamayuru, tiny houses like an open accordian concert into each other. Lower down, sullen, fast athwart runs the river, its icy source being at the holy lake of Manasarovar. A mighty river, the Indus, giving to India its name, its thousand-mile meandering mingles with myth and legend before debouching into the waters of the Arabian Sea.

Buddhist invocations to the gods permeate the atmosphere—on prayer-flags fluttering in the breeze, or the *mani*-stones piled high or the stupas that dot the land. The stupa is a monument, shrine and repository derived from the Buddha's tomb and has come to symbolize existence. These structures which guard the approaches to habitation in the Buddhist parts of the Himalayas are usually atop a square red base, signifying the earth. A large white dome

After the odyssey comes a fairy-tale ending. A fort, a palace and a monastery stand out against the sky, amidst an avenue of poplars. This is Leh. The journey has just begun. As the Buddhists say: 'When you are ready, the teacher will appear.'

Above every village, large or small, rise the ubiquitous *gompas,* turreting the pristine air to break the articulate silence of the land of Vajrayana, the Vehicle of the Thunderbolt. Dominating life in these desolate places, built as acts of piety, believing in what are known as the Four Noble Truths, Sakyamuni discovered that man's existence is inseparable from sorrow; the cause of suffering is desire; peace is achieved by extinguishing all desire. And your liberation lies in following the *Ashtangika Marg*—the Eight-fold Path.

'Good walls make good neighbours',

admonished the poet, but here where there is no habitation you will still find yourself walking into walls. The visitor constantly sees what are little more than dents on the surface of the desert. More real than walls in the mind, these *mani*-walls too are dedicated to the glory of god. If you look carefully, engraved in Tibetan script is the eternal invocation: *Om Mani Padme Hum* (Hail to the Jewel in the Lotus).

The *gompa*, or more simply the monastery, is placed at the spiritual center of the Buddhist

Shey gompa: Fourteen kilometres from Leh, Shey was once the ancient capital of Ladakh and it continued to be so after Sengee Namgyal moved out to Leh to build the palace there in the 17th century.

Thikse gompa: It lies above the village, right at the end of the road. The newer temple to the right with the new image of Maitreya—sitting in the lotus posture on an upraised throne—was dedicated in 1980 by His Holiness, the Dalai Lama.

Interior of Thikse monastery. Religious ceremonies in the monastery are preceded by the playing of long horns. The complex contains numerous wall paintings, noted among them being the fresco of the 84 Mahasiddhas.

way of life. Built on a hillock or on a slope above the village these are homes for celibate monks. At the very summit of the *gompa* and of the religious hierarchy lives the Rinpoche, or the chief Lama of the order. Numberless *gompas* are scattered over the land. Some of them are:

Spituk gompa. Built in the 15th century, the *gompa* stands on a solitary precipice just eight kilometres from Leh above the village of the same name.

Facing page: Cham *or masked dancers performing at the Hemis festival, celebrated once every 12 years at the Hemis Gompa, 49 kms from Leh. The ritual dances are performed to ward off evil and bring prosperity.*
Following pages 38-39: *Kang Yisay Peak (6,400 m), Ladakh.*

Hemis gompa: Forty kilometres from Leh lies the best known of all the *gompas.* The fame of its dance-festival, held here every summer, has travelled far and wide. You do not see it till you are almost there, tucked away in a dale in the Zanskar Range. Those devil-dances, the drums, the percussion of cymbals and trumpeting horns give the place a certain mystique. Dedicated to Padmasambhava, it houses a very special treasure, open to the gaze of the public once every eleven years—a rare *thangka*, not like the ones you normally see, but embroidered with pearls: It is by far the richest and largest of all *gompas*, founded, we are told, in the 1630s under the benevolent patronage of Sengee Namgyal.

On the other bank of the Indus is the village and religious sanctuary of Alchi, the oldest of

monasteries in Ladakh. Legend has it that the monk Rinchen-Zang-Po (the Great Translator), pressed a dry twig into the ground, promising to build a monastery if the stick sprouted. And it did. A huge tree grew. You can still see its stump in the ground. History books would have us believe the monastery was founded in the 11th century by Kal-dan Shes-rab, a nobleman of Tibet who moved to this region to resist the tides of Hinduism and Islam. Its unique art forms have a distinctive Tibetan

grown, and in some places apricots. Trees are scarce, so wood is hard to produce. There are many sheep, especially very large geldings; their flesh is most excellent and their wool extraordinarily fine. Musk deer also exist. In valleys at the foot of mountains, and also near streams, the natives find a good deal of gold, not in large nuggets, but as gold dust. They eat meat, and the flour of roasted barley, and drink Chang, a sort of beer made from barley.

Stok in Ladakh. Two monks race along the roof tops and terraces of the monastery, as though in a mad trance. After the trance breaks, they will become sacred oracles assiduously consulted by the faithful.

flavour. Paintings cover every available inch of space.

Alchi stands as a tribute to the cosmic vision of its nameless builders, those old followers of the faith who turned their backs on all else for no reason other than the pursuit of their own beliefs. Here they moved to live unmolested by the strident religious stances building up in the north and south. Alchi has survived the upheavals of history to serve as a constant reminder of the final triumph of the human spirit. Among Western visitors who came here was the twenty-nine year old Italian Jesuit, Ippolito Desideri. He observed:

It is mountains, sterile, and altogether horrible. Barley is the chief product; a little wheat is

One need not emphasize the astuteness of Desideri's observations. Some of these are true even today: the mountains are barren; roasted barley is washed down with Chang. Desideri had an empathy for the Ladakhi—a quality which was to hold him in good stead as he went on to Tibet and lived there for five years. Ladakh beckons those who love the mountains and its incomparable sense of space plus the inherent freedom of wide open spaces, and the growth and learning processes that develop from sticking it out. As they say:

*'It is not true, it is not true
that we come to live here.
We come only to sleep, only to dream.'*

Ever tried walking for two or three weeks with

not a soul in sight? Try the wild mountains of Zanskar if you like to give up all hopes of seeing human habitation ever again. Then you'll suddenly find yourself stumbling upon an oasis. The flavour comes from the remoteness, a tang absent in other remote areas. Zanskar is not for the faint-hearted. It takes a bit of daring—you might be tempted to start all over again. But no. This is a trip not meant to be repeated except in memory—over and over again.

As you cross the icy waters of a river, hanging

of the Kali Yuga, as all universal beliefs wane, there, hidden in the silence of the mountains is still a place where the faithful live out their humble lives following the faith in Zanskar.

HIMACHAL

'I hurried still more not to miss the vision for which we had come so far. Then the miracle happened. Folded in light mist, hill after hill rolled away into the distance from beneath my

Stok. The Lha (oracle) is about to begin his dance, in which he will work himself into a trance so that he can predict the future.

on to the tail of a mule—for the mule knows the river better than any man and knows where to go—memories of the lush vale of Kashmir will seem like another day. In this stark remoteness you are on your own. Except at the end, where the twin peaks of Nun (7,135 m) and Kun (7,087 m) announce the end of the Zanskar.

The Tibetan influence on this region is apparent in the presence of fluttering prayer flags, the faces of the people, the *chortens*, the stupas and the *gompas*. For more than a thousand years, the region was under the control of the local dynasties of Zangla till it fell to the rulers of Kashmir.

Subsequent to the disturbances in Tibet and the resultant exodus of faith, this remains the last bastion of what Tibet must have been like for ages before it fell. Take heart. In the dark age

feet, and over this green ocean sparkled the vast icebergs of the Himalaya's!' exclaimed Lionel Terray as he fell in love with the magic of the Himachal Himalayas. 'Never in my remotest dreams had I imagined such beauty could exist on earth . . . Time effaces all memories, but the feelings of that moment are branded in me while I live. . . . Looking back today I see more, that it was not only the revelation of my dreams of youth, but the beginnings of an experience which has influenced me more than almost any other—the discovery of a world outside our time', he panted of this love at first sight.

It is that kind of a place.

Another other-worldly experience is to set one's eyes on the scintillating paintings of the Russian emigre, Roerich. Lodged at Naggar in Kulu, the artist turned his back upon the social

whirlwinds of his time to paddle his solitary canoe. Huge deodars line the path to this shrine for the initiated. Nicholas Konstantinovich Roerich was a man of immense talents, delighting in the company of fellow-theosophists like Anne Besant and Bishop Blavatsky. He was the only European in the Kulu valley to achieve world fame. This, coupled with his retaining a touch of regal royalty, did not exactly endear him to the sahibs of the Raj. He turned towards the mystical East. On facing the snowy ramparts of the globe, the Himalayas, his genius seems to have sounded a cosmic note. Over seven thousand paintings flowed from his magical hands. He passed away peacefully in Kulu as the frost of December began to show its jagged teeth in 1947. On a terrace below the hall is a little memorial:

15th December 1947
Samvat 30 Magh 2004 Vikram Era
The great Friend of India
Maharishi Nicholas Roerich
The Last Rites were performed here
OM RAM

The relentless boom of a tortured river reverberates in a narrow gorge. Along the banks of the Beas, the road etched into the very face of the sheer rocky scarp falls like a curtain in a straight plumb-line into the milky foam down below. Not for the faint-hearted is the twenty-five mile trek along this ribbon of a river, for from the warmth of cloistered Mandi, you will soon find yourself in Kulu—the valley of the Gods.

Down the ages, lost travellers have rediscovered themselves in a unique world—abounding with festivals and fairs. Indeed, there are numberless temples, innumerable gods, deities and *devatas*. Make no mistake, the last alone number over three hundred and fifty and dominate all social life here.

Of course, the highest in the pantheon is Lord Raghunath, followed closely by the various *devatas* who are revered after *rishis* like Vyas, Kapil, Vashisht, Gautam, Dhaumya, Kartikswami, Markandeya, Shandil and Jagdagan.

The gods here are as numerous as the ancient Greek gods: Devi Hadimba of Manali; Devi Phugni of Dughi-Lag and Sarvari Valley;

Facing page: *The gods on* palkis *(carriages) en route* through the village.

Devi Tripura Sundari of Naggar; Devi Ambika of Nirmand and Shamshar Mahadeva of Ani, all belong to the outer Saraj while those who dwell in the inner Saraj are Sharinga Rishi of Cheeni, Devi Durga of Goshaini, Pandir of Sainj and Jogni Bajhari of Jalori range. Durbasa Rishi and Narad Muni belong to the Rupi valley.

But no aloofness for these gods, they are as human as you would like. They do not stay away from those who believe in them, but are active participants in the life of the community. And each one has parents, brothers, sisters and relatives scattered all over these very mountains. If they are happy, they eat and drink and are merry, but if neglected, they can frown upon lesser mortals and wreak havoc all around.

Whatever happens, no one forgets the *devis*. Annual *jatras* are held to appease the gods. On a specially appointed day, the *rath* (chariot) is decorated as befits them—scarves, flowers, ornaments and finally masks are put on for a procession to the fair. With a deep-rooted belief in the power of the gods, oracles are consulted when in doubt. The gods speak through the 'gur', and no one dare question this exchange.

Sometimes, the *devatas* visit each other, with an entourage of devotees. The host village throws open its doors to warmly welcome the guests. Tremendous is the influence of the gods in these mountains. It makes for a people who are essentially simple, honest, god-fearing, unmoved by the pressures of an acquisitive way of life and rooted firmly in the bedrock of the past. It has served them well and they serve it in this way.

What could be a better place for fairs and festivals? Should you find a crowd of bedecked residents moving en masse over the hills to another village, you can follow them confidently as *mela*-time is on. Each village has one or two fairs a year. Each village god is worshipped in his own area.

Himachal Festivals

The largest festival remains the week-long Dusshera festival of Kulu, closely followed by the Budhi-Diwali at Nirmand. This last takes place a month after Diwali in the plains, a special highlight being recitations from the great epics in the local dialects. Dusshera is celebrated with great gusto, for it symbolizes the victory of good over evil.

All paths in the valley lead to but one place—the Dhalpur Maidan—where the hill *devatas* come in grand procession to pay their respects to Raghunathji. And before you, on the grassy maidan, stretching atop the precipitous cliff above the river, the *doli* (palanquin) of the gods comes alive, swinging from side to side, as man tries to still it—to no avail. Despair is at a pitch as the angry gods do not relent. The crowds mill around the sacred craft. It parts for an old priest, who makes his way, barely

the road to the temporary abode of Lord Raghunath. And though the journey is small, a mere stroll really, the sheer grandeur defies the written word.

For the next five days, all the rituals of the gods are followed most meticulously at both dawn and dusk. Then on the last day, the *rath* is taken to a sacred grove on the river bank where a huge pile of grass and wood awaits the final rites. It is set alight with much merriment just as Lanka was set ablaze in the days of the

Priests taking the palanquin of Lord Raghunathji to the Dusshera grounds in Kulu.

touching the *doli*, and goes into a trance, muttering some words. In a trance, possessed by the gods, all listen to the priest's predictions with bated breath: 'Hailstones will wreck the apricot-blossoms. You've not paid homage to your household gods, O fool!'

What stuns the first-time visitor is the sheer scale of it all: priests, followers, palanquin-bearers, standard-bearers, musicians and just bystanders. Indeed, all roads lead to the maidan.

On the first day, the chariot of Lord Raghunath is bedecked with flowers at the old temple of Sultanpur. Some chants from the priest and then the perambulations begin. First come the priests, followed by the descendants of the Raja of Kulu.

As the sun begins its slow descent, it is time for the sacred task of pulling the chariot across

Ramayana. After sunset, Lord Raghunath returns to the main temple astride his wooden palanquin.

Of course, the festival just cannot begin till the arrival of the omnipotent goddess, Hadimba, the chief deity of Kulu, worshipped most respectably as 'Grandmother' by the Rajas of Kulu. You will find her ensconced at Ramshilla on reaching Manali.

Dusshera in the Kulu valley has little to do with the tradition of the *Ramayana*, unlike in the plains. In the mountains, under a waxing moon, it celebrates the arrival of the image of Lord Raghunath from far off Ayodhya.

Come autumn and Kulu's charm beckons all. From Naggar to Manali is a superb walk of some twelve miles. As you start, the lush valley is a mile broad but tapers through terraced fields to end up at the Rohtang Pass. At Sarsei is the 17th century temple dedicated to Krishna. And if you wander off the road a little you'll stumble upon the village of Dashal where rising thirty feet in the air is the Gaurishankar temple dedicated to Shiva and Parvati. At Ganjan is the temple of Dochamucha, a mini stone structure in the middle of a grove of deodars. These are the twin images of the Rai of Rupi.

Today's Jagatsukh was once called Nast, the capital of the old kingdom of Kulu before it was moved to Naggar. Around Jagatsukh remains of

picturesque grove of ancient deodars, some of them over a thousand years old, this sacred grove stands protected on account of a strange order. 'Some of them were cut down and removed for timber a few years ago,' writes Justice G. D. Khosla, 'but a somewhat eccentric Scottish member of the Indian Civil Service fortunately stopped further depredation by issuing an order that the deodars were ancient monuments and, therefore, protected under the Ancient Sites and Remains Act. No one

Priest bathing Lord Raghunathji.

earlier temples and fortresses abound, bringing back memories and signs of a time, over a thousand years ago, when this was the capital of a flourishing kingdom.

Manali was originally a small hamlet called Dana—a final stop for muleteers to pick up some fodder before crossing the bleak Rohtang. Duff Dunbar, a Scotsman, came here in the middle of the 18th century as a Deputy Forest Officer. Building a house for himself in true *pahari* style near the village of Dunghri, he lived here, one with the locals. With personal funds he built the first suspension bridge at Bunthar with the devotion of a visionary and planted the fabulous forests in the area.

A little way off is the famous grove temple of the goddess Hadimba, who married Bhim and is revered in the Manali region. Set in a

challenged the legality of the order and the trees were saved.'

Good luck to posterity!

Ancient inscriptions date this 80-foot high temple to AD 1553. The pagoda-style wood and stone structure has seen many repairs and echoes of a Buddhist past still linger on.

Rohtang Pass

The Rohtang Pass at 3,985 metres lies at the very end of the Kulu valley, separating it from the valley of Lahoul. The river Beas rises near the Rohtang pass. The pass acts as a barrier to

Following pages 46-47: *Mt. Kinnaur Kailash, which lies between the Punjab Himalayas and the Garhwal Himalayas.*

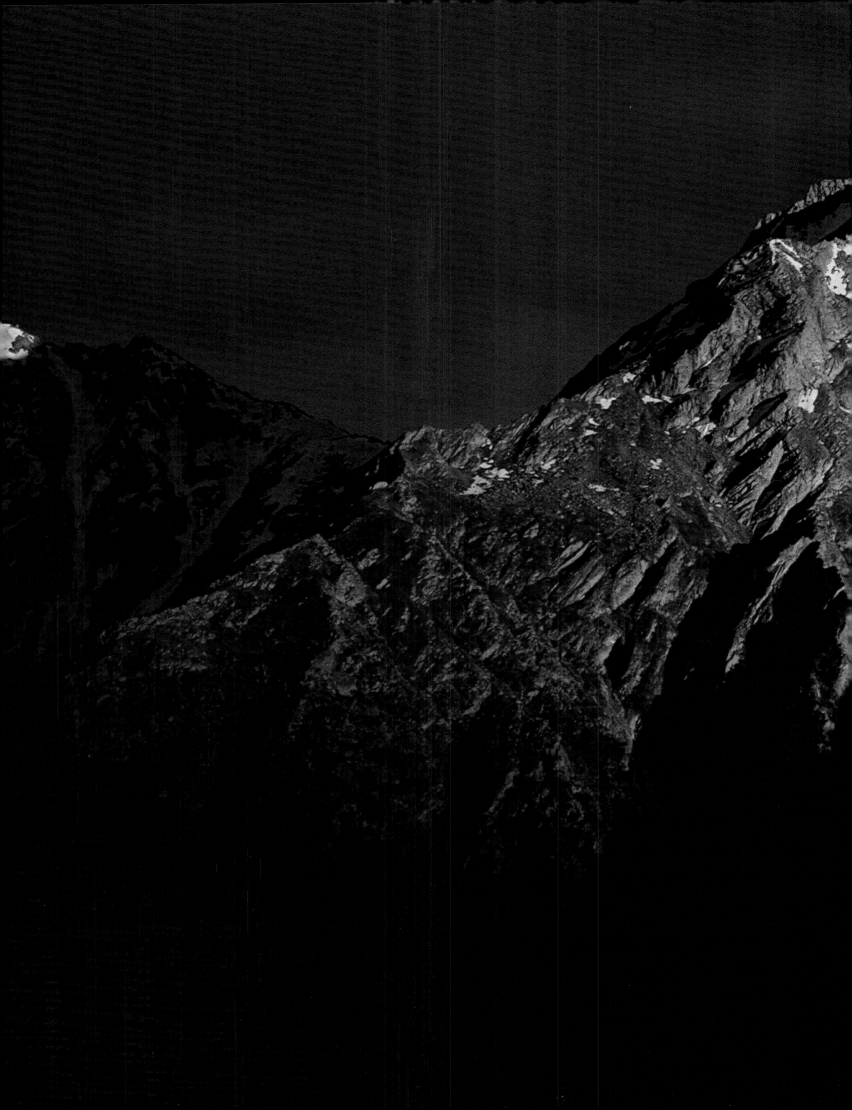

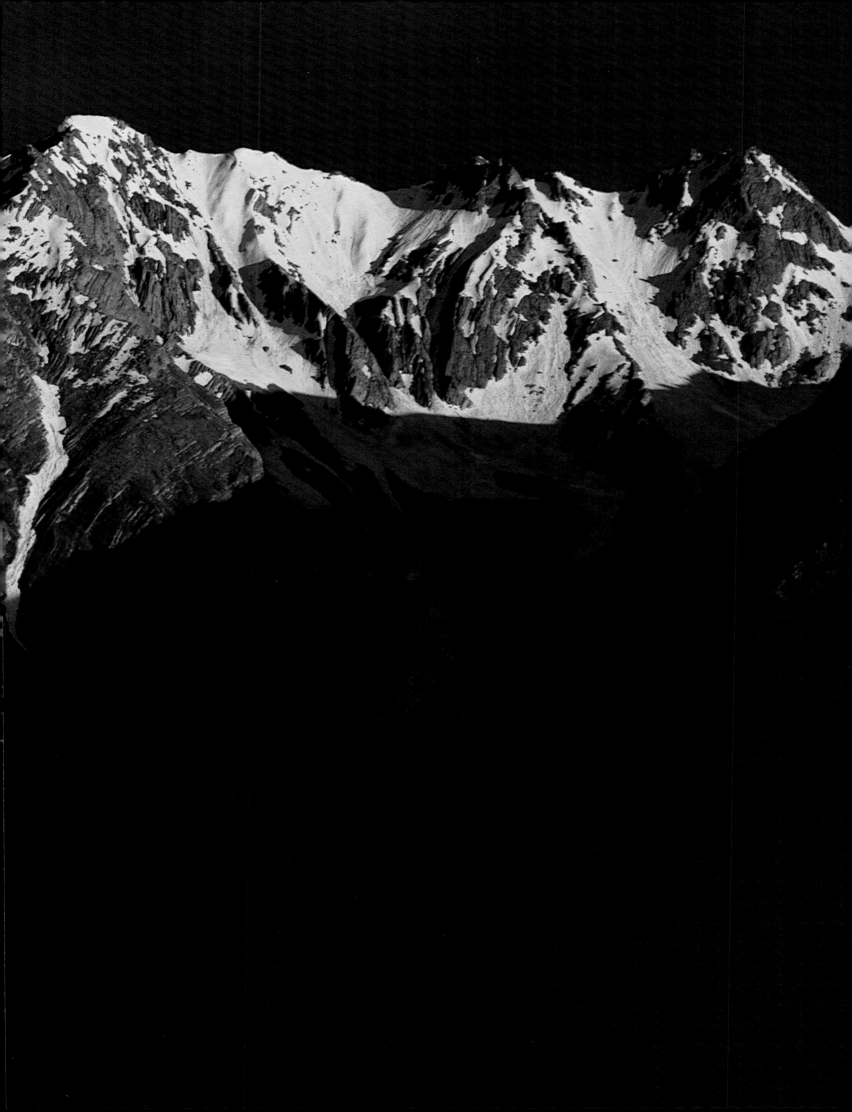

the monsoon for the region of Lahoul. It is considered the opening to the heavenly higher Himalayas and remains a favourite of the courageous who have a taste for the forbidden world of wilderness and for the unknown. Opening to traffic in May, it has now become easy to get here.

The 34 km stretch of the Rohtang pass has remained a source of fascination for the traveller. Wrapped in legend, this rock-strewn path which, incidentally, gives the pass its

Tibetans and succeeded in throwing them out and seizing Lahoul. By the turn of the century, Raja Man Singh ruled over both sides of the pass. Then in 1840, the Sikhs over-ran the place, taking in their stride the twin valleys of Kulu and Lahoul.

From the pass one can get spectacular views of precipitous cliffs, deep ravines, large glaciers and moraines. Once accessible only between July and October, now the pass is open even in May as cross country routes are being

A chorten announces the approaching habitation in a beautiful tract of Pin Valley, Spiti.

name, is like a lodestone for those who seek newer horizons.

According to legend, the pass was created by the charismatic Tibetan chief, Gyafo Kissan, who used to travel from Ladakh to Bhunter in a single day. One day he was in a great hurry, spurring his steed and impatiently lashing the mountain top with his whip to get through faster. The Rohtang was born as a result of one of his whiplashes. In later years, Tibetan raiders trooped down the pass many a time to get to the Lahoul valley, but like their yaks, they never could get used to its warmth.

According to history, in AD 1125, Lha Chen Utpala conquered Kulu and took tribute from Raja Sikander Pal. A treaty was hammered out, which stayed in force well into the 16th century. At this point in time, Bidhi Singh took on the

developed, and skiing is also possible above the pass. The summer months of May and June are the most colourful and popular, while July to September are considered the best months for high altitude treks over the Rohtang Pass and on to Lahoul, Zanskar and Ladakh.

En route to the Rahala Falls are a series of dark orifices on the face of the mountain through which one can feel the very cold draft as it seems to rush through hidden ducts from atop the peaks. Should the orifices begin to whistle, it is said, it's time to get away from the Rohtang.

Beyond the last ridge lies the vast amphitheater of the Himalayas. How much history these remote places must have seen—the brave Moravian missionaries and their blushing brides, traders from Tibet, the spy-masters of the Great Game, or pioneers like Moorcraft?

At the top of the pass, near the headwaters of the Beas, just a little way off is the mystical lake of Dashair where, we are told, Akbar the Great's troops let a horse stray so close to the waters that it drowned. The putrefying carcass polluted the holy water, and, it is said, till the offending body was not removed, the Emperor's daughter continued to suffer from an inexplicable bout of illness. Yes, in the Himalayas, facts are stranger then fiction.

Simla, sprawled against the sky, came up as

of a place and is now the capital of the hill-state of Himachal Pradesh.

Chail, unlike Simla, has regal origins. What was once just a clump of trees was gifted by the British to Maharaja Bhupendra Singh of Patiala, who, having been externed from Simla for certain indiscretions, resolved to turn his back on it and build his personal hill-station here. Rajgarh palace was converted into a luxury hotel that has few rivals. A serpentine road leads to the hill-top, through winding, mossy deodar-

Ki monastery is the largest in Spiti, and houses 300 lamas. It has some rare paintings and sculptures.

a hill resort towards the early 19th century. Officially, the British were invited here to help throw out the marauding Gurkhas, which they did after three years. A certain Lieutenant Ross is credited with building the first house, a thatched cottage built from local timber in 1819. He was followed by Captain Kennedy in 1821. Guest-houses, paying-guests, hotels and hoteliers were to come up much later. Among these were the Hotel Cecil and Clarke's. In the wry words of Emily Eden, the main attraction of the hill-station was its climate: 'The sharp clear air is perfectly exhilarating. I have felt nothing like it—I mean nothing so *English* . . .'

Or it could be that it was a good place to get away from the seething crowds of the plains to carry on the great charade of being *really* British. Simla has always been an officious sort

shaded paths. The best time to be in Chail is autumn when the place is awash with dahlias, hydrangeas, fuchsias, gladioli and canna. The Military School here boasts the highest cricket ground in the world at 7,656 feet.

'It should be—unless they've begun to play cricket in Tibet!' grumbles an old watchman. 'Doesn't the ball go over the edge and get lost?' 'Sometimes—in the mist of the monsoon!'

Nahan, in the lower foothills, is an easy drive through the valley of the Doon. To the north, some twenty-five miles as the crow flies, are the Chur Ranges of the Himalayas, where Vigne, a well-known traveller, was a guest of Major (as he was then) George Everest, Surveyor-General of India and the first man to scale the mountain which came to be named after him.

Chapter 3

GARHWAL-KUMAON

The mighty range that lies between the river Tons in the west and the Kali in the east is known as the Garhwal-Kumaon Himalaya. Venerated since times immemorial, this range has been a place of mystic beauty and sublimity. The ancient poets of India looked northwards and said:

He who thinks of the Himalayas, though he should not behold them, is greater than he who performs all worship at Kashi. And he who thinks of them shall be forgiven all his sins, and all things that die on the Himalayas and all things that in dying think of his snows are freed from sin. In a hundred ages of the gods I could not tell you of the glories of the Himalayas where Shiva lived and where the Ganges falls from the foot of Vishnu like the slender thread of the lotus flower.

Why are these particular mountains holy? There are no stock answers. Maybe it is because nowhere else do they dominate the lives of the people with such a degree of visibility. Seen through the eyes of the early travellers, the Garhwal-Kumaon ranges continue to defy the written word as they stun the senses by their sheer grandeur. In 1888 Sherman Oakley wrote:

I have seen much of European mountains but in stupendous sublimity combined with a magnificent and luxuriant beauty, I have seen nothing that can be compared with them. Although none of the summits reach an elevation equal to that attained by a few of the peaks on other parts of the chain, for only two of them exceed 25,000 feet, it is probable that the average elevation of the snowy range of Garhwal-Kumaon is

nowhere surpassed. For a continuous distance of some 200 miles the peaks constantly reach a height of 22,000 to more than 25,000 feet.

Here, then, is a place for all reasons and all seasons. For its charm permits the trekker or climber to move ever so slowly to the top of those ice-topped peaks and to come down to alpine valleys carpeted with wild flowers.

One such valley was given its name by Frank Smythe in 1931. I took a magical trip there. My eyes were blinded by the brilliant colours of a valley that wears a quilt of finely embroidered flowers. I stood and stared, wide-eyed and speechless. Flowers of every imaginable colour and hue; the air was so saturated with scent that clouds of fragrance, wafted by a gust of Himalayan breeze, stormed the senses.

'*Kyon sahib . . . kya hua?*' (What's happened, sahib?) The robust voice of our guide intrudes in our reverie. The spell is broken. But the magic lingers, working a different kind of spell this time.

'*Yeh hai . . .* Valley of Flowers!'

The Valley of Flowers! Arriving beyond Joshimath, Smythe left the banks of the Alaknanda and entered the Bhyundar valley. He fell in love with the lush meadows of this botanists' paradise and made it known to the world. Primulas of subtle shades, wild geraniums, saxifrages poking out of rocky crannies, red and yellow potentillas, star-kissed anemones, violets, dog-roses, all these and much more flourish here.

'Impossible to take a step without crushing a flower!' Smythe had exclaimed. And there are other places in the Garhwals where the hills are rich in flora—the Har-ki-doon, Hursil, Tungnath, Chandrashila and the Khiraun valley where the balsam grows to a height of eight feet—but at the end of the monsoon, the Bhyundar has a concentration of flowers unmatched elsewhere. It would be no

Facing page: *The beautiful holy city of Deoprayag, Garhwal, at the confluence of the Bhagirathi and the Alaknanda rivers, which meet here to form the Ganga.*

exaggeration to call it one of the most beautiful valleys in the world.

The awed village-folk, with a hint of fear, will tell you of nights when the mountain-fairies tend this garden by the light of a million glow-worms. A garden at the Gateway of Heaven, watered by Heaven's own sacred fount—the Pushpa Ganga, or the River of Flowers.

The drive into the land of the fifty-two forts of Garhwal is on a road that runs along

reasonably comfortable but just fifty years ago, Smythe had observed:

So they venture on their pilgrimage . . . Some borne magnificently by coolies, some toiling along in rags, some almost crawling, preyed on by disease and distorted by dreadful deformities . . . Europeans who have read and travelled cannot conceive what goes on in the minds of these simple folk, many of them from the agricultural

Women pilgrims bathing in the hot sulphur springs of Gauri Kund, near Kedarnath, Garhwal.

the river. The typical mountain village, its rough stone houses straddling the spur of a hill above the fields, is off the beaten track and attracts few outsiders. There are usually half-a-dozen families belonging to the village, each family possessing a few acres of land on which everyone works. Women join in the ploughing, sowing, weeding and reaping. Sometimes women are the only ones working in the fields. It is not that the men have run away. They have joined the exodus from the hills to take jobs in the plains or join the army.

But faith keeps people going in these hills. As the mountains are the mystical dwellings of the gods, a magnetic pull draws pilgrims to this, the highest of pilgrimages. Nowadays a journey is

parts of India, wonderment and fear must be the prime ingredients. So the pilgrimage becomes an adventure, unknown dangers threaten the broad well-made path, at any moment the Gods, who hold the rocks in leash, may unloose their wrath upon the hapless passerby. To the European it is a walk to Badrinath, to the Hindu pilgrim it is far, far more . . .

Look at the names that lend themselves to this place: Tapobhoomi (Land of Meditation), Badrikashram (the Hermitage), Devbhoomi (Land of the Gods) and Himavant (Land of the Himalayas).

Tucked away in the heart of the four riverine valleys of Garhwal are the four holy sites (*char dhams*) of pilgrimage: Yamnotri,

Gangotri, Kedarnath and Badrinath. Situated over 10,000 feet above sea level, glacial chill reigns supreme here for six months in a year. Traditionally, the pilgrimage begins in mid-April and the portals of the shrines close to the pilgrims in November. If you move deeper into the mountains, away from the foothills, the pine gives way to the oak, the oak to the rhododendron and pine, and finally the birch stands like an obelisk at the very end.

the Second World War, got away in a garbage cart from an internment camp in Dehradun, are linked with this valley. Crossing over from Kharsali, they were beaten back by the weather. But renewed attempts took them up to Uttarkashi, where they were locked up by the police in Bhatwari. Escaping through a ventilator, they reached Tibet and freedom. Later, Harrer wrote the best-seller *Seven Years in Tibet* after becoming a political aide to the Dalai Lama.

Oblations by bride at Gangotri.

'Never hurt a tree. You know not when you might need one to lean on', goes an old proverb in the hills. And the conifers, aloof and silent, continue to shrug the snow off their shoulders, in affirmation of life.

The peak above Yamnotri is named Kalinda, another name for the sun. Yamnotri is the source of the Jamuna. In 1820, Bailey Fraser, probably the first travel-writer to get thus far, noted: 'The spot named Yamnotri is, in fact, very little beyond where the various streams, formed on the mountain brow by the melting mounds of snow, unite in one and fall into a basin below. Down the ravines are seen trickling the numerous sources of the Jamuna . . . '

The escapades of Heinrich Harrer and a companion, two prisoners-of-war who, during

Birth of the Ganga

Once there was a king called Bhagirath, whose ancestors, 60,000 in number, were reduced to ashes by a curse. The devout king did penance to bring the Ganga down from the heavens. But the mighty river feared that if she gushed down to earth, all would be destroyed by her torrential trip. Shiva, the God of Creation and Destruction, agreed to receive her in the mighty tangle of his hair and then release her gently.

The king mounted his chariot and rode ahead of the waters to the spot where the ashes of his ancestors lay. With him came a procession of gods, nymphs, demons, ogres and

Following pages 54-55: *The gods ready for a journey.*

53

sages. Wherever the chariot went, the river followed meekly in the wheelruts of his chariot wheels and all of creation bathed in the holy waters, which wash away all sins.

. . .

A professional mountaineer like Eric Shipton came to Gaumukh in the summer of 1934 and was so moved that he wrote:

It was impossible to be unmoved at the sight of the torbid flood rushing from the black ice cave under the towering wall of ice which marked the end of the Gangotri Glacier, and to reflect that here, where it was a bare thirty feet wide, the Ganges began a journey of fifteen hundred miles to the Bay of Bengal into which it poured through many mouths, one alone full twenty miles wide.

When one further reflected that from sea to source it was regarded with veneration by more than two hundred million beings, who, in life, believe that to bathe in it is to be cleansed from sin, and at death ask no more but their ashes may be cast upon its waters, it has a combination of stupendous spiritual and physical marvels which could hardly be equalled elsewhere in the world.

This was not the only place Shipton came to that year. In 1936, he was to find a way up towards the Nanda Devi group, explore the passes between Badrinath, Gangotri and Kedarnath, climb Maiktoli. Yet what stood out was the river of faith!

En route to Gaumukh is the town of Uttarkashi. One of the few survivors of the past is a quaint bungalow at Hursil, the home of the British freebooter, Frederick E. Wilson. Arriving here in the middle of the 19th century, Wilson leased entire forest tracks from the Raja of Tehri and floated timber down the river to meet the never-ending demand for the tracks for the railways, which were still in their infancy.

His fortunes soared from eight lakhs in the first year to forty-five, and then to the charmed figure of a crore. He acquired the nickname 'Pahari' (hill-dweller) Wilson, as he completely identified with the hills of Garhwal. Pahari

Wilson married the daughter of the drummer of Mukba and settled down to raise a family in the hills. Bridge-building was another of his ventures. These bridges were meant to facilitate travel to the shrine at Gangotri. The most well-known of these was the one over the Jadhganga near Bhaironghati, over 1,200 feet above the young Bhagirathi as she thunders through a deep defile. This shaky contraption was at first a source of much terror to the locals. To reassure people, Wilson mounted his horse and galloped to and fro across his bridge. The bridge has long since vanished but the locals will tell you that the hoofbeats of Wilson's horse still echo on full-moon nights.

In the other riverine valley is the most voluminous of rivers, the Alaknanda. There are many who insist that this is the real Ganga. So all controversies end when the waters of the Alaknanda merge with the Bhagirathi at Deoprayag where the Ganga begins.

Upstream is the sombre town of Srinagar, where the first Europeans to arrive were the famous uncle-nephew team of painters, the Daniells. Not till 1796 would another European set foot in those mysterious mountains to the north. The next to come was Thomas Hardwicke who was a botanist.

At the end of the Mandakini valley is the temple of Kedarnath in the center of a wide open valley. The simple stone structure belies the brilliance of its architects, who bonded huge stone slabs with lime and mortar and concealed iron clamps—hallmarks of the genius of Adi Shankaracharya. He strode these mountains like a colossus, barely thirty-one years old, as he completed the task of rejuvenating Hinduism before passing on to the other world. A simple monument behind the temple marks the spot where he took *samadhi*. Looming larger than life are the temples all over Garhwal and Kumaon, testifying to the genius of the great saint.

As you walk down the mountain, past anemones strewn like stardust among bare rocks, the peal of temple bells and murmur of a gurgling stream, you can hear a pilgrim

Facing page: *A snowbound Gaumukh (the birthplace of the Bhagirathi Ganga) with the Shivling (6,544 m), known as the Indian Matterhorn, standing sentinel over it.*

humming a quartet of Tulsidas, the immortal poet of the *Ramayana*:

When every single plant appears to be God's own plant,
When every single rock appears to be God's own image,
When every stream appears to be God's own stream,
Only then does God become pleased and reveal Himself within.

At Gopeshwar, the headquarters of the border district of Chamoli, the only sound is the roar of the river, straining and foaming to break loose from the constraining mountains. At times, it is barely a touch away, then suddenly round the next bend it is lost in a submontane gorge. For those who like to ski, the alpine slopes of Auli beckon just a few kilometres away while the pilgrim is drawn to the ultimate pilgrimage: Badrinath.

In winter, the Badrinath establishment moves to Joshimath. On the great Kumbh day, it is said, Vishnu himself appears to the believers atop Nil Kanth peak. The sky is ablaze with lightning and thunder serenades the ranges. As camphor perfumes the air and bells tinkle, if you look through the lifting mist you too will ask: Could it be the lightning playing tricks?

. . .

'Can you suggest a simple trek? You know . . . some place one can get to without loads of equipment, rock climbing or crossing galciers and getting lost.' Innumerable times this question keeps popping up from people of all ages, both young and old, who would like to get a feel of the high mountains without wandering off into a world of icy wastes.

Luckily there is such a place and those who can pack their bags between April and October can surrender themselves to the wonderland of the Central Himalayas. Lost amidst the oak and

Facing page: *Madmaheswar Jee (at 3,030 m), one of the important* panchkedars *(five temples) in the Rudra Himalayas. The Shiva temple is believed to have sprung up where one of the five parts (the stomach) of the shattered Nandi Bull—Shiva's mount—fell on earth.*

maple, the rhododendron and the deodar are the enchanted waters of unspoilt Dodital.

Hurry it up a bit, though. For if the plans to build a road right up to the lake's edge are really implemented, then all the magic will vanish.

You too will fall in love with 'the smell of the Himalayas—composed of rotting pine-cones, damp wood-smoke and dripping undergrowth', as Kipling defined it. Four hundred kilometres from Delhi—with a walk of just twenty—and you'll be at your destination. The serpentine hill-road stretches from the banks of the Ganga at Rishikesh, the dwelling of the hermits, through the lower hills and down to Uttarkashi. The place has lost much of its innocence, what with regular earthquakes rattling the town awake. This is the last pick-up point for whatever you might have forgotten behind; and if you'd prefer to walk the trails unencumbered, porters are readily available.

Hitch a ride or hire a jeep up to the road's end at Kalyani. Then you are well and truly on your own, without the 'civilizing' influence of man and his ilk.

On a clear autumnal day, all you'll hear is birdsong if not the thumping of your own heart. Hadn't you forgotten it was even there? To cool off, the inviting waters of the many mountain-torrents gushing by will do just fine. Tumbling through the mossy-floored forests are the many sounds of silence, broken, if at all, by the chatter of black Himalayan pheasants or the doleful song of the green barbet.

The climb to Agora knocks the wind out of you: a climb of two-and-a-half-thousand feet in a bare five kilometres and not a blade of grass for shade. At high noon, the clouds swirl over-head, as a thin translucent veil of mist settles down. A night's halt at the old Forest Bungalow will refresh your spirits and at the crack of dawn, one is ready to take to the path before the sun blazes once again.

The fatigue of a 15 km walk is washed away by the first glimpse of the still waters of Dodital. These three acres of water are a deep emerald green or, as in Garhwali, 'dodi-coloured'.

'Fortunate is he who can spend some days among the Garhwal-Kumaon Himalaya', said a sage of yore. And far, far away from human presence one can discover oneself as one takes a solitary walk along the sedge.

Look, the words of Walt Whitman begin to echo in the mind:

> *'I believe a leaf of grass is no less than*
> *the journey-work of the stars,*
> *And the pismire is equally perfect, and a*
> *   grain of sand,*
> *and the eggs of the wren,*
> *And the running blackberry would adorn the*
> *   parlours of heaven,*
> *And the cow crunching with depressed head*
> *   surpasses any statue,*
> *And a mouse is miracle enough to stagger*
> *   Sextillions of infidels.'*

For the more daring there are numberless lakes, large and small, waiting to be rediscovered in the vista of the Central Himalayas.

Mussoorie

'Who goes to the hills goes to his mother!' Not till they were at least a mile up in the sky did the British colonials feel fully refreshed. Finally, the scorching sun and the choking dust of summer was behind them as the breeze soughing through the pines brought back a flood of nostalgia—it *was* just like home.

The hill stations of Mussoorie, Nainital, Ranikhet and Almora came into being around the 1830s. What began as small settlements grew into large stations to turn into the hill-stations of today. Mussoorie was not named after a place in England. The British were content to follow the name given by the hill-folk. Growing in abundance was the Mansur shrub (*Coriana nepalensis*). You can still see the hardy bushes growing in places where few plants would dare take a foothold.

A.P. Barron of Shahjehanpur stumbled upon the waters of the Naini lake and Nainital began its saga. Memories of the British Isles abound in these hills as many of the properties of yesteryear still bear the names of those who built them, though the houses have changed hands many times over. The magic of the old names still lingers.

Take our house, for instance. It is simply called 'Trim Lodge' (with Trim Cottage and Trim Ville just below us in quick succession on the same spur). Try as hard as I would, there was no trace of a Mr. Trim. Could he have been a friend of Colonel Young, the founder of Mussoorie, who came from the Irish county of Trim? From the record room I could only establish that the last European owner was a certain E. H. Cockburn, who left the property to his sister by a will executed in her favour. She passed away soon after and the property devolved to the Custodian General, who put it on the block.

All over the hills, those hardy pioneers built houses with whatever could be found locally. The lime-kilns of Khattapani produced all the lime and mortar from which the old buildings were built. The rhododendron trees, now lost forever, were used for beams and rafters.

Above Trim Lodge, on a flat atop a ridge is Mullingar—the oldest building in town—its ruinous look buttressing the claim. It was a shooting lodge built by a youthful Captain Young, who lived in Dehradun, raising the Gurkha Battalion after the Battle of Nalapani. He spoke fluent Gurkhali and was a hit with his troops. And what is 'Mullingar'? It's the name of the town he came from and returned to, in his old age, as General Young.

Undeniable nostalgia must have dogged the footsteps of those early visitors as you still find houses with Scottish names: Glenbrook, Gorgehead, Scottsburn and Redburn. The hill-stations were great places for clubs, fancy fairs and dances. Here under the eaves lonely bachelors met grass-widows whose husbands had better things to do in the plains like propping up the affairs of state. Himalaya Club was one such place, established in 1841 with a membership of one hundred and forty-eight.

Another famous club—the Happy Valley Club—was acquired by the brewer, V. A. Mackinnon in 1904. A decent place, replete with a reading-room, a library, card-rooms and a billiard-room. A skating-rink, then reputedly the largest of its kind in Asia, was built in 1890 by one Miller, a dentist. But the venture floundered. Excellent samples of colonial architecture are the early churches in the hill-station, built for the spiritual needs of those pioneers. What takes one's breath away is the sheer brilliance of the stained-glass windows. They are living testimony of days when innocence was a virtue and the Sandman had to wait for another day.

. . .

It was left to Eric Shipton and H.D. Tilman to open up the successful exploration of the Garhwal-Kumaon Himalayas in 1934. Both were coffee growers in Kenya, on farms 160 miles apart, who got in touch in 1929. On Eric's plantation was a 200 ft high tooth of

than nine attempts had been made to penetrate the basin or to set foot on 'the pearl of the Central Himalayas'. Of these early attempts, Hugh Ruttledge wrote:

Nanda Devi imposes upon her votaries an admission test as yet beyond their skill and endurance: a 70-mile barrier-ring on which stand twelve measured peaks over 21,000 feet high, and which has no depression lower than 17,000 feet, except in the west

The temple dedicated to Nanda Devi, the supreme goddess of the Garhwal Himalayas, is located in Lata Village, which lies 25 miles on the trekking route from Joshimath to Nanda Devi Sanctuary.

granite, an inconvenience on a farm, but a blessing to those who loved climbing. They began their first climb on this jutting rock face in Africa and laid the foundation for one of the most famous of mountaineering relationships.

In January 1934, the pair got in touch again to make a combined attempt to ford the Rishi gorge. Shipton found a devout follower in Tilman. The meeting resulted in a trip of five months in the company of three Sherpas in the Himalayas at a cost of just £140 including fares out and back to England in a cargo vessel!

The main object of the trip was to discover a route into the inner basin at the foot of Nanda Devi, the 'inner sanctuary', to make a fairly accurate map of it and to find out if the mountain could be climbed by a larger party.

We must remember that since 1883, no less

where the Rishi Ganga, rising at the foot of Nanda Devi and draining an area of some 250 square miles of ice and snow, has carved for itself what must be one of the most terrific ridges in the world. Two internal ridges, converging from the north and south upon this river, form as it were the curtains of an inner sanctuary, within which the great mountain soars up to 25,660 feet.

Hugh Ruttledge is in the forefront of those early commissioners of Kumaon who had a feeling for the place and followed in the footsteps of able administrators like Traill and Atkinson. E. Sherman Oakley wrote in 1888: 'None of the Kumaon summits reach an elevation equal to that attained by a few of the peaks.' The *Gazetteer* of 1888 makes special mention of the remoteness of the place: 'It appears like a spire of greying rock sprinkled with snow and lying to the north-east of Trishul and north-west of Nanda Kot and rising far above the similarly snow-clad summits which surround it. The summit is altogether inaccessible. The natives maintain that smoke is sometimes seen to issue from its summit which they regard as the kitchen of the local deity.'

To the locals, Nanda Devi is the benevolent

the summit and the girl died suddenly of complications from a hernia. An iron plaque placed in the south sanctuary meadows in her memory quotes from the diary of Nanda Devi Unsoeld: 'I stand upon a wind-swept ridge at night with the stars bright above and I am no longer alone but I waver and merge with all the shadows that surround me. I am a part of the whole and am content.'

It is that kind of place. Especially if you take the trail to Roopkund, the mystery lake which

Bedni bugyal (meadow) at 3,550 m. A rare view of the alpine meadow, usually shrouded in mist, which is used as a summer pasture.

mountain goddess, a mother who can grant boons or destroy those who stray from the chosen path. In the hills, people tell stories of how Trail, the first commissioner, was struck blind because, disturbed by the festivities of the pilgrims, he had moved the Nanda Devi temple from near his office in the Badhan Fort to Almora, and that he regained his sight only when he begged her for forgiveness.

The cult of Nanda Devi is shared by one and all in these mountains. Yet the most grief-stricken story unfolded during an expedition in 1976 led by the irrepressible Willi Unsoeld, who had brought along his twenty-two year old daughter whom he had named after the mountain. She was young, blonde and beautiful, working for the Peace Corps in Nepal. Tragedy struck at Camp IV, just below

is known to keep its visitors in an icy embrace for eternity. Most people say only fools step in where angels fear to tread. Sometimes it is wiser to go the way of fools if only to prove that *you can* when most of us can't . . . The gentle dwellers of the mountain valleys of Uttarakhand, almost resigned to their fate, say '*Deb key maar, nah khabar nah saar*' (When the gods strike, there is neither logic nor reason).

At Wan, the last village on the trail, a hundred families manage to wrest a living from the calcinated soil and lead a happy life. Above Wan lives a survivor of the Indian National Army, a hero of the National Movement, living on tales of battles in lands abroad, and lost in a collection of dog-eared novels. Hidden close by in a sacred grove is Latu, the mischievous herald of the hill goddess, Nanda Devi. If one were to go by the folk songs sung in her honour, she is forever stirring up trouble. So wary are the people of the goddess, that the doors of the shrine are opened only on special occasions.

What gives the visitors goose-pimples is the truly eerie setting of the shrine: a stupendous hoary tree, with each branch larger than a full grown deodar, all festooned with moss and lichens together dangling in the air, making the

mystery lake drains the last bit of our energy. Along the rim of the lake lie scattered skeletal remains, triggering a lively debate on their origin: wandering nomads, Tibetan traders or even General Zorawar's army in retreat!

The clouds triumph again. One snow-flake meets another. A waltz begins. The lake freezes over once again—keeping in tight wraps its icy secrets for yet another day. Or age.

. . .

Chaukhamba Massif (7,164 m) in Garhwal (chau, four; khamba, pillars) which gets this name from its flat, roof-like profile, with four pillar-like peaks.

nerves tingle as Latu's magic weaves an unseen but palpable web.

Beyond the tree-line, the high-altitude meadows of Bedni and Aali Bugyal beckon with an ambrosial air and form a path to the borders of heaven.

Fact and fiction merge into each other like swirling mists. The waters of the Nandakini are never used for oblations anywhere in the high mountains. It has been so ever since the ill-fated Raj Jaat Yatra of King Yashdawal, many centuries ago, to the Nand Devi. Though warned against it, the king had insisted on going for the *yatra*. The villagers believe that the waters got polluted when the straw, on which the queen lay while giving birth to a child in a bleak cave above the river, fell into it.

One last haul up a couple of zig-zags to the

Next time the smog, the dust and heat get to you, don't throw up your hands in despair as you weave your way through the traffic. Just a few hours away there is a place where you can take a deep breath of that diamond air and be whole again.

It is to one of the early commissioners of Kumaon, Sir Henry Ramsay, that Binsar owes its beginnings. Atop a spur he built his residence alongside the court. The house is no longer a house, just a memory of the four years from 1852 to 1856, when Ramsay pioneered education in this region. From village to village, astride his horse he travelled with

Following pages 64-65: *Four peaks—Trishul, Devasthan, Maiktoli and Nanda Devi—viewed from Pithoragarh district in Garhwal, bordering Nepal.*

determination to bring progress to the area and his work was not in vain.

It is not always just 'love and fresh air' in the mountains. As I came down the mountains towards the hills of Garhwal, 'Environment — Toy of the Rich!' was the graffiti painted along the road above the roaring river valley. Unless timely measures are taken to protect the interests of those who live here, one can get caught up in a losing spiral at the end of which is he whom we seek to help: the common

snow is spread out on a canvas of two hundred and fifty miles and not too far away in the distance either. As the crow flies, it is a bare sixteen miles away.

The Anashakti Asram straddles a spur above the quaint bazaar beyond the bus-stand and is the place to which Mahatma Gandhi came, to recuperate, in 1929.

Should you want to go further, there's always the short haul to Baijnath just twenty kilometres away where the old temples

Reflections in rain water puddles, Bedni.

man. At times, its all so easy, this euphoria that deludes us into thinking that reserved forests are some kind of 'special sanctuaries'. We would do well to remember that they exist solely by democratic decree.

There are many walks you can take around Binsar. Jageshwar is 25 kilometres away and is famous for a superb group of temples; over a hundred and fifty, dating to the ninth century AD. You could spend the night at the tourist bungalow, set against a frieze of tall, brooding deodars. Remember to take time off to wander around as there's always a bus to take you back to Almora, 34 kilometres away.

Another place that has impressed itself on my memory is the little world of Kausani, just 50 kilometres away from Almora. A vista of

beckon, or you could go on to Bageshwar, on the confluence of the Gomti and Saryu rivers. The priests of this valley are famed as astrologers. You too could find out what's in store for you!.

Lakshmi Chand, the titular ruler of Kumaon, built the Lachmeswar temples at Bageshwar and Almora to keep the Gods on his side and made grants to the other great temples, including Jageshwar in 1602. Lakshmi Chand finds mention in Jehangir's *Memoirs*: 'The hill-prince brought a great number of the valuable rarities of his mountains for my acceptance. Amongst them were beautiful strong ponies called *gunths*, several hawks and falcons, numerous pod of musk and whole skins of the musk-deer with the musk in them. This Raja is the richest hill-chief, and it is said there is a gold mine in his territory.'

Strange were the ways of kings. We are told that a line of villages stretching from the snows to Almora were set apart for supplying the royal table with ice. The supply of ice was obtained in the mountains, from where it was despatched by porters to Damras on the Yamuna, where it was packed in boxes and carried by raft on the Yamuna to Daryapur reaching Delhi in three days and nights.

fame were to come his way as he turned naturalist.

Purnagiri, dedicated to Bhagbatti, the goddess of Plenty, is visited by thousands of pilgrims each year. The climb to the highest shrine is for those favoured by the Gods while the lower one is open to all. Legend has it that a stubborn sadhu struggled to the top oblivious of his co-travellers. The angry goddess flung the offender to the other side of the glacier-fed river. Banished forever, it is said, he continues

Signboard at Rudra Prayag indicating the spot where Corbett killed the famous man-eating leopard which had stalked the region for eight years between 1918-1926.

Pithoragarh still retains the flavour of a rustic backwater where the excitement of the day is a visit to Rai Gufa—the Pataal Bhuvneshwar. Travelling from east to west, it is easier to exit through Tanakpur to take in the magic of the little known towns of Champawat and Lohaghat. Champawat's claim to fame rests on the legendary Jim Corbett, born in 1875, the son of the postmaster of Nainital.

Corbett grew up in the forests around Koladhungi, a small village in the Terai. He was a master story-teller and wrote of his adventures in books which became bestsellers. Worldwide recognition and

his worship to placate the anger of the Gods, two thousand feet high in the sky.

For a true flavour of the world of Kumaon, walk off the beaten track and you might just meet an old-timer who has heard of stories that are found in books—of the epic struggle between man and the elements. The Kumaon Mandal Vikas Nigam is one of the best organized tourist infrastructures in the country. Its bungalows, big and small, are an oasis of delight. Should you be among those of the adventurous variety, stay at one of the old dak bungalows of the Raj and who knows, you might have a really exciting stay—something to write home about!

It was around 4:30 a.m. on 29th May 1965 that Phu Dorji, Rawat and myself left the last camp on Everest at a height of approximately 28,000 ft. The winds shrieked, flaying us mercilessly. We dug our ice axes in and kept cutting steps but the higher we went the fiercer the wind blew.

Slowly and cautiously we negotiated the big boulder of the South Summit. We did not go over the top but took a traverse to the left about 70 ft below till we came to a narrow gulley in the snow, which we named India's Den. This gulley is on the main traverse from the South Col to Hillary's Chimney. Descending vertically for about 35 ft we came to a narrow path that led us to the Chimney—an almost vertical obstacle between rock and snow crevice which I had dreaded ever since I was selected for the expedition. Phu Dorji, who was ahead, tried climbing but kept slipping. He would cut a step with the ice axe

View of Mount Everest (centre).

and gingerly place his foot on it but would slip all the same. His abortive attempts disheartened me till at last I saw him swing the ice-axe into the wall on the top. It held there with the axe driven in fully. Helped thus, he slowly crossed the Chimney. He asked Rawat to come up another way, from the rock side. Rawat too slipped and had to be pushed while I, who followed them, had literally to be pulled up. In fact, negotiating the Chimney proved to be a most hazardous effort. Breathing, which had never been easy, became ever more difficult. We would take a deep breath but it would shorten into a hiccup. We were gasping for breath. Would the ascent never end? Time and again I wondered if our quest was worth this terrible ordeal. But each time mind overruled matter and I found myself taking yet another step. The humps undulated endlessly. Sometimes there would be only rock or shoulder of snow. I kept asking myself how much longer and how much farther. On every climb one is assailed by these doubts, and there comes a time when the mind and body begin to

Base Camp at 17,800 ft.

Camp I (20,000 ft).

En route *to Camp III at 23,000 ft.*

Camp at South Col. (26,200 ft).

ASCENT TO MT. EVEREST

H. P. S. Ahluwalia

dwell on the sheer bliss of going downhill again. I was in such a state. Yet, another part in me urged me to go on. It couldn't be more than a few feet now—perhaps fifty or even less. But the slope led on and on. Heavens, was there no end? And then, suddenly, there *was* an end. No more little humps, only a white little dome curving slightly above us. Incredible! It was the summit of the Everest. Yes, we were there. Linking arms, we climbed the last few feet together. The tricolor planted by our first summit party was fluttering in the air, tattered but jaunty. There were other flags too and some souvenirs and offerings left by the summit parties which had been here before us. From this point, there was a

sheer drop and I looked into space. It was freezing, maybe 30 degrees below zero, but suddenly the wind dropped, and I remember thinking: This is a special gift from the Goddess Mother of the Earth. We surveyed the panorama from the highest point in the world. We sighted Makalu and Lhotse, Nuptse, and Kanchenjunga on the horizon, and many other peaks, all far below us. We gazed north towards the Tibetan plateau, and south towards the plains of India. The roof of the Thyangboche monastery glistened in the distance, an

On top of the world at 8,848 m.

upturned mirror, floating, as it were, on the opal mists of the morning. The view was unforgettable. Of all the emotions which surged through me as I stood on the summit looking over the miles of panorama below, the dominant one was humility. The physical in me seemed to say, 'Thank God, it's all over!.' The spiritual in me experienced a sense of loss for having done the 'ultimate' in mountaineering. Thereafter there would be nothing higher to climb and all roads would lead down. In this moment of triumph, I thought of all the Everesters who had come before us and those who would follow us. The British, the Swiss, the Americans, and my own countrymen. I thought of the few who had tried and triumphed, and of the many who had tried— and failed.

Crossing the crevice in ice fall area.

Towards Camp II, 21,300 ft.

The final assault.

View of Tibet from the top of Mount Everest.

Photographs Courtesy: S. S. Singh, Capt. M. S. Kohli

Chapter 4

❋

NEPAL

Nepal is not hard to locate in any map. It appears as a long narrow rectangle hedged in-between the Himalayas to the north and tapering off to the base of the foothills in the Terai. These moist wetlands to the south are densely forested and with a bit of luck you'll still be able to spot a leopard, tiger, rhinoceros or elephant. Seldom rising over 6,000 feet, these lower hills constitute the last bastion of wildlife against the rapacious instincts of humans. To the north rises the natural barrier of the Mahabharat ranges, which have been effective down the ages in keeping out wanton intruders.

As you reach the top of these ranges, a sheltered valley is spread out in front of you and in the distance the towering Himalayas heave to the north. The Chinese traveller, Huien Tsang, trudged through the valley in AD 637 and wrote:

The kingdom of Nepal is in the middle of the snowy mountains. Its soil abounds in fruits and flowers and the climate is cold. The inhabitants are of a hard nature, and neither good faith and justice appeals to them, but they are gifted with a very considerable skill in the arts . . . The houses are of wood, painted and sculptured; the people are fond of bathing, of dramatic representations, of astrology and bloody sacrifices . . . Buddhism and Brahmanism flourish in the principal temples, which are wealthy and well-supported. Commerce prospers and trade is well organized and directed.

The Kathmandu valley sprawls over an area some 50 miles in breadth and over five hundred miles in length. To approach the giants rising in the north, the route is via the riverine valleys. What a stunning array of

Facing page: Clay Bhairub image, representing the ferocious aspect of a divinity.

peaks: twenty-five over 25,000 feet, two of these over 28,000 feet and three over 27,000 feet. Through this impenetrable barrier three rivers have carved their way by cutting across the crest zone, etching in their wake dark gorges and in the process dividing the kingdom into three parts.

If you start from the east, the Kosi river takes into its ambit the border between Sikkim and the Langtang and the whole sweep of Kanchenjunga, Everest, Makalu and Cho Oyu range. The Po Chu carries the waters from the watershed of Tibet and becomes the Sun Kosi. In the middle or the central section are the dark, swirling waters of the Kali Gandaki and its numerous tributaries spanning the Ganesh, Himanchuli, Manasalu and Annapurna ranges. Then, in the west, flows the Karnali taking in the ranges, including Dhaulagiri. From this point on, the titans taper off as they meet the Garhwal-Kumaon Himalayas.

The very early history of Nepal is wrapped in the mist of antiquity. It is said the Kirantis ruled the place in the first century BC. With three-fourths of the country's population dwelling in the Kathmandu valley, it is this particular valley which held the reins of supremacy. The Mallas, who were Hindus, held sway from the 13th to the 18th centuries. Yet their religion was no impediment to their unstinted support to the art and culture of the predominantly Buddhist Newaris. From the three centres of Kathmandu, Patan and Bhaktapur, three brothers ruled the land, vying with each other in creating works of glorious beauty, which constitute a feast for the senses even today. Foremost among the Newari customs that has come down to us is the worship of a young virgin as Kumari, the living incarnation of the goddess Taleju, the patron deity of the ruling family.

The Mallas are credited with having built some of the finest temples and palaces. It was to their court that the great musicians and poets flocked. Those were idyllic days, almost too good to be true. Historically, it was to be just the proverbial lull before the storm. For two decades small skirmishes, battles and wars raged between the twenty-four hill states of the Gurkhas, better-known as the *Chaubisia-Raj* or 'the rule of the twenty-four'. Then in 1769, Prithvi Narayan Shah consolidated his power and marched upon Kathmandu. Arriving during the Indrajatra festival in the fall, he was blessed by the Kumari as he asked the show to go on. The Malla king simply fled in panic. The foundations of the Shah dynasty had been laid. The golden age of Nepali renaissance had come to an end. It was followed by a period of turmoil as the Gurkhas began their long march into neighbouring Tibet, Sikkim, Kumaon and Garhwal.

Foremost amongst the tales of Gurkha valour is the one relating to the Battle of Nalapani. Nalapani is a small hillock in the valley of the Doon where two invaders, the British and the Gurkhas, were to meet each other for the first time. The date: October 31, 1815.

Today in the wide vale of Dehradun, you'll come upon a war memorial unique in the annals of war, for it celebrates the bravery of both victor and vanquished! As one poet said: 'Another step-by-step will cover the living imprint of your feet/But you, yourself should not distinguish between your victory and your defeat.'

The murmuring waters of the Rispana refuse to tell this tale of over a hundred and seventy five years ago. Yet it was these very waters that were to hold the key to the crucial Battle of Nalapani whose outcome would, in turn, give birth to twin developments: the arrival of the descendants of the honorable East India Company to Garhwal and the setting up of the Gurkha Regiment.

In autumn the Rispana is no longer in spate. Reduced to a trickle, it bares its boulder-strewn teeth across a causeway which is easily crossed. 'In the end is my beginning', said the poet. And they did in the end what they should have done in the beginning—but hindsight makes wise men of us all, forgetting for once that when the dogs of war are afoot, the first victims are good sense, vision and reason.

Fall of Nepal

So was it on a mellow autumn morning of October 31, 1815. Two conquerors literally bumped into each other here. The Gurkhas, who had been in Garhwal for twelve years, now held the small fort of Kalinga near Nalapani, situated on the highest point of a low spur about three miles northeast of Dehradun. The hill itself is no more than five hundred feet high and is very steep—except towards the south where the fort was built—and was then, as now, covered with a thick forest of sal trees. The tableland on the top is about three-quarters of a mile in length and was protected by an irregular fortification which followed the form of the ground in its structure. There were only some three to four hundred of the regular troops of the Gurkhas present under the command of Balbhadra Singh Thapa, a nephew of Amar Singh, who commanded in Garhwal.

When the British sent a messenger at midnight to demand the surrender of the fort, he found Thapa enjoying a well-earned repose. The commander read the letter, tore it up, giving no other answer than that it was not at all customary to receive or answer letters at such an unreasonable hour. But he sent his *salaams* to the English Sardar, assuring him that he would pay him a visit in his camp.

Colonel Mawby thought next day to punish this insolent barbarian, and mounting a couple of 6-pounders and two howitzers on elephants, proceeded to take the fort by assault. But a few rounds later, the task was given up as impracticable and the troops returned to Dehradun with less contempt for the enemy and a more just appreciation of what really lay ahead.

Three weeks later, on October 24, General Robert Gillespie took command of the force. After careful reconnaissance, orders were given for an immediate assault. Fascines and gabions were ready beforehand, while all 12-pounders and howitzers and half the 6-pounders were sent atop elephants to the tableland. This was occupied without any opposition. Batteries were soon ready for the guns, and four separate storming parties were ordered to be ready for the assault.

In the meantime, the Gurkhas had done everything possible with the limited men and materials at their disposal. The wall, although not yet complete, was raised sufficiently to render scaling impossible. All the gaps were filled up with stones from the riverbed, stockades were erected along the lines of approach, and a gun was placed which enfiladed the principal side of attack.

The British guns played on the fort for some time, but did little damage—and 'this, perhaps, uniting with the eagerness of a sanguine temper, induced General Gillespie to give the signal for assault some hours sooner than it was intended.' In the resultant confusion, three out of the four columns took no part in the attack.

The assault commenced at nine in the morning and the stockades were easily carried, but on approaching the walls, the British suffered severely in both officers and men. No ladders were forthcoming for a time, and the obstacles were then found to be too great to be overcome. The troops were obliged to retreat under shelter of a village in the rear. Gillespie then led in person three fresh companies of the 53rd Regiment and had barely reached the spot in front of the wicket, 'where, as he was cheering on his men, waving his hat in one hand and his sword in the other, he received a shot through the heart and fell dead on the spot.' His aide-de-camp, O'Hara, was killed beside him and many other officers were wounded.

Colonel Carpenter, who succeeded to the command, deemed it prudent to retreat to Dehradun and there wait for further reinforcements. The gun at the wicket had done much damage to the attacking party. Several persons penetrated to this very wicket, but, unsupported, could produce no effect. A very heavy fire was kept up from the walls by the garrison and showers of arrows and stones were discharged at the assailants. Many severe wounds were received from stones, which were thrown very dexterously: the women, too, were seen occupied in throwing them, regardless of exposure. Five officers were killed and fifteen wounded, of whom several died subsequently of injuries then received. So ended the first assault on the petty fort of Kalinga.

It was not until November 24 that the arrival of a siege battery from Delhi enabled the British to resume the attack on Kalinga. The Gurkhas made a gallant and desperate defence, standing themselves in the breach whilst using every missile that came to hand: balls, arrows and stones. The second time round, the English were taking no chances. They advanced in a cool and self-possessed manner; a few got to the crest of the breach and fell there, but the majority remained below, exposed to a murderous fire. 'No one turned to fly, but none went onwards; they stood to be slaughtered, while their officers exposed themselves most gallantly and unreservedly.' Thus the disastrous results of the first attack were repeated—and it was only now discovered that there was no water within the fort! The besieged had to get water from a spring at some distance from the walls. Arrangements were at once made to cut off this water and the fire from the batteries recommenced the next day, doing great damage from the unprotected state of the garrison and the shattered condition of their defences.

On the night of November 30, only three days after the adoption of the measures (which were equally feasible a month earlier) Balbhadra Thapa with 70 men—all that remained of his impregnable garrison—evacuated Kalinga. Within the fort, 'the whole area . . . was a slaughter-house, strewn with the bodies of the dead and the wounded and the limbs of those who had been torn to pieces by the bursting of the shells; those who yet lived piteously calling out for water, of which they had not tasted for days.'

The determined resolution of the small party which held this small post for more than a month against so comparatively large a force must surely wring admiration from everyone, especially when the horrors of the latter portion of this are considered: the dismal spectacle of their women and children thus immured with themselves; and the hopelessness of relief, which destroyed any other motive for the obstinate defence they made. Was it not the result of a high sense of duty, supported by unsubdued courage. This, and a generous spirit of courtesy towards their enemy, certainly marked the character of the garrison of Kalinga during the period of its siege. So, far from insulting the bodies of the dead and wounded, they permitted them to lie untouched till carried away; and none were stripped, as was universally the case in those days.

We are told that while the batteries were playing, a man was seen on the breach, advancing and waving his hand. The guns ceased firing for a while and the man came into the batteries. His lower jaw had been

Boudhanatha stupa, situated to the east of Kathmandu, has the omnipresent eyes of Buddha painted on it. The brightly painted eyes (and the nose that looks like a question mark) are supposed to represent the Buddha's ever-watchful gaze.

shattered by a cannon shot, and he came ever so frankly to solicit assistance from his enemy. Of course, this was readily given; and, when discharged from hospital, he expressed his desire to return to his corps to combat the British again!

The fort of Kalinga was razed to the ground before the troops left and there is not even a light unevenness of ground to mark the spot where the great Battle of Nalapani once took place. All we have are two small mouments; one in the memory of Sir Robert Rollo Gillespie and the officers, non-commissioned officers and soldiers who died there, and the other in memory of Balbhadra Thapa and the gallant Gurkha defenders of the fort.

The Gurkha wars ended with the Treaty of Sangauli by which a part of the Terai was given up to the British. Nepal retreated into a state of isolation and the British Resident in Nepal found himself very lonely in his new compound, in an abandoned corner of Kathmandu.

The seventy-years rule of the Shahs in Nepal was to be challenged by the arrival of a zealous army officer, Jung Bahadur Rana, who waded through a bloodbath to the throne after he massacred every member of the royal household including anyone who might have some day challenged his authority. The Kot massacre, as this came to be known, wiped out not just those who may have one day risen in revolt but also all the good administrators in the kingdom. Rana also left a legacy for his descendants whereby they would become hereditary prime ministers under a titular monarch who would always be beholden to them.

Some of the most incongruous architecture seen on the Kathmandu skyline is a gift of the reign of the Ranas. On consolidating their power, they travelled to Europe, picking up at random bits and pieces and transplanting them on some of the finest structures built by the discerning Mallas. Of course, other Westerners had been to Nepal in the days of yore. In the

1660s, two Jesuit priests, Johan Grueber and Albert d'Orville, had made a journey from Peking to Kathmandu. Leaving China in April 1661, they arrived in Nepal the following year in spring. Then, in 1769, in response to an appeal from the Raja of Nepal, a small party under Captain Kinloch was to make rudimentary sketches of the border that lay to the south.

Those early surveyors, the *pundits*—part explorers, part spies—had to wait till 1873 to

According to legend, the Tree of Paradise or the Kalpa-Vrisksha, taking the form of a man, was wandering around the lanes of the old city when an observant bystander recognized the great wonder. He got a hold of the tree and would not let go of it until he had wrested the promise of getting another tree, large enough to build a house. The struggle between the two lasted for quite some time till the tree relented and granted a boon. That, we are told, is how Kathmandu happened to

Samye festival held at Hanuman Dhoka every 12 years.

put in an appearance. Hari Ram of the Survey of India was one such man who was undaunted by the risky task of wandering into forbidden lands in disguise. He walked along the gorge of the Kali Gandaki discovering fossilized ammonites (called *shaligrams*), whose worship formed an integral part of Hinduism in the Himalayas.

The rule of the Ranas came to an end in 1951 with the abdication of the last Rana prime minister and the return of King Tribhuvan from exile in India.

A new dawn had begun in Nepal.

KATHMANDU

Kathmandu, the capital of Nepal, was known as Kantipur as late as the 16th century.

have got its name: *kath* means wood and *mandu* means house.

Over two thousand temples are scattered around the valley and are a tribute to a god-fearing people. So thorough has the mingling of Hindu and Buddhist faiths been that any attempts to classify them is bound to be fraught with nothing more than frustration. This unique blend has produced a crucible of faith in the Himalayas where the pagoda-styled dome sits most comfortably atop a temple. For the believers there is no confusion. Indeed there are some which are easily identifiable like the holiest of holies, Pashupati Nath, which draws the devout, as it stands out on the right bank of the Bagmati with a gigantic bronze bull guarding the portals of faith. It is to this temple that the

royal family of Nepal retires to worship the gods.

On the opposite bank, on the other side of the river is the Guheswari temple. There is no image there, but the devout throng the riverside with offerings which they continue to pour through an opening on the front. Swayambhunath sits atop a hillock at the end of some four hundred steps and the eyes of the Buddha keep a watch on the valley. Legend has it that this, the largest of stupas, owes its origins to the efforts of a libertine woman who prospered as the years passed. In her old age, she was inspired to build a monument large enough to house 'the Mind of all the Buddhas'. But there was no land and she decided to approach the king. Impressed by the desire of the woman, the king granted her permission to build a stupa on land as large as an ox's hide.

Using the cunning she had used to survive in the past, she cut the leather into thin strips, laying them along each other in length till she covered the present area and then with the money she had acquired over the years, she began to build this great stupa. The courtiers were not amused. They did their best to put a stop to this. But the king was adamant: he had given his word. And Nepal's grandest stupa rose towards the skies.

Pilgrims flock here from far and wide turning it into a Tibetan festival at times of prayer. Thus it has been for over two thousand years. While at Patan live those great artists who, since the times of Ashoka the Great, have used their skills to turn wood, metal and stone into objects worthy of the gods. Have no doubt about their abilities, just a cursory glance at the exquisite workmanship of the Krishna temple will dispel all clouds of doubt as scenes straight out of the *Mahabharat* and *Ramayana* come to life.

Facing page: Mt.Everest (8,848m) straddles the border between China and Nepal. The main peak of the Himalayas is also the highest in the world. The Tibetans call it Chomolungma, or Mother Goddess of the Earth, while in Nepal it is known as Sagarmatha (Mother of the Universe).
Following pages 78-79: Mt. Ama Dablam (6,856 m), Nepal, which has shops selling trekking equipment. The name means 'Necklace of the Mother'.

Should you be looking for more, go to Bhaktapur. In this city of devotees are the famed treasures of Malla rule. The renowned gateway of the Taleju temple has aptly been called 'the most lovely piece of art in the whole kingdom' while the Durbar Chowk remains a lasting tribute to the rule of the Mallas.

Everest

Of Everest, the great peak, the highest of them all, much has been written. In the old maps it was simply marked as Peak XV. The Tibetans call it Chomolungma, meaning Mother Goddess of the Earth. Popular accounts have a breathless official of the Survey of India, George Everest, bursting into the office of his superiors exclaming: 'Sir! I have just discovered the highest peak in the world.' And he was right. The height was calculated to be 29,002 feet and it was to fall in 1953 to Sir Edmund Hillary and Tenzing Norgay. The feat was announced to the world on the day of Queen Elizabeth II's coronation.

But who was Everest?

He came out to India as a young cadet in the Bengal Artillery in 1806. As an assistant to Colonel Lambton, the founder of the Great Trigonometrical Survey of India in 1818, he was to find both his vocation and his avocation. After twelve years, in 1830, the East India Company appointed him as Surveyor-General, a post from which he was to retire in 1843. Most of the work he had set out to do was done and the real memorial remains the great meridian arc of India, passing from Cape Comorin to the Himalayas.

Another illustrious luminary of those hoary days was a certain Lieutenant-Colonel Frederick Young, an Irishman from Mullingar, Senior by four years to Everest, he was the civil and military officer of the Doon valley. The account of their running dispute is a study of the typical British stiff upper-lip behaviour.

At one time Everest took umbrage to being addressed as 'Compass-*wala*', in those days a common term used for all who turned up in the plains of India with odolites and compasses. Young wondered how the term could cause offence. But even then, he gave

instructions that in future all official correspondence must refer to him as 'Surveyor-General-Sahib-Bahadur'. Not one to be satisfied too easily, Everest said that while he was aware no offence was meant, to keep the record straight he must from now on be addressed only by his proper title, 'Surveyor-General Kishewar Hind'.

Aylmer Jean Galsworthy reveals an exchange of correspondence between the two. Subsequently, Everest received some

command saying that he did not notice anything disrespectful, 'compass *wala*' being the designation commonly used for the Survey of India in this part of the country and, 'if for a moment I could have supposed it likely to give offence I should have ordered it to be corrected. I feel convinced that no disrespect could have been intended on the part of the petitioners, because they could not possibly gain anything by this insolence . . . I have given directions that no public document

Sunset on Mt. Everest.

papers regarding his pension, which still referred to him as '*Kumpas Wala*'. He was livid and dashed off an indignant note: 'I am *not* a Kumpass Wala but Surveyor General and Superintendent of the Great Trigonometrical Survey of India. These are the appellations by which my masters address me, and no person has a right to withhold them from me.

'As I never apply nicknames to any other persons, and studiously avoid giving offence to others, I have a right to look for equal courtesy in return, and I hope you will prevent such offensive epithets appearing in any public paper intended to meet my eye, or wherein I may be spoken of.'

Young replied with all the tact at his

shall pass my office in which you are designated by any other title than Surveyor General Sahib Bahadur.

'I never entertained the belief that you intended me any offence', relented Everest. 'I objected to a low, familiar, appellative which, though it may be in common use in the bazaar, I cannot allow to be applied to me as my official designation. The Commissioner . . . always designates me in his *parwanas* . . . by the title of Surveyor-General Kishewar Hind, which is a literal translation of that assigned to me by my masters. I shall be obliged by your adopting that designation.'

With the 'battle of titles' barely behind them, trouble cropped up from an unexpected quarter—this time it was objections from rich households over surveyors climbing vantage points from where they got a stunning view of the *zenanahs*.

Everest complied with the request, which he still found most ridiculous, that 'the Surveyor should withdraw to a less convenient situation, where he might build a tower to any height he liked. The cost of the move would be paid for. The Zamindar must have money in superfluity to be willing to incur so vast a charge for an object so insignificant as that of removing ten or twenty paces . . . an edifice

Survey is a department of hard work and not idleness . . . and men who sit up all night and all day, with barely time for sleep or meals, have rarely leisure for such trifling as Zalim Singh anticipates, even if their tastes were so ill-regulated, and their lot so forlorn, as to become a prey to speculative amusement.'

In 1832, Everest got special permission to move a part of his office to the cooler climes of the hill-resort in order 'to establish themselves at Mussoorie and fix them until

Annapurna II peak (7,937 m) in Nepal at sunset.

which, since it must surpass all circumjacent dwellings would equally command a view of his *zenana* for people disposed to be impertinent and curious at the distance of quarter of a mile.

'But the persons of the Great Trigonometrical Survey are of too good taste to concern themselves with Zalim Singh's *zenana*, and he does not do them justice.'

The tone of mockery is clear as he adds: 'Persuaded that our telescopes which invert have magic powers, and are able to turn women upside down (an indecent posture no doubt and very shocking to contemplate), it is natural enough that they should assign to us the propensity of sitting all day long spying through stone walls at those whom they deem so enchanting. (But the Great Trigonometrical

such time as the two northern sections of the Great Arc are brought to a satisfactory termination.' At Hathipaon, 7,080 feet above sea level on the main spur three miles west of the new township, he moved to a property known as the Park.

The place was to give him more problems than pleasure—the road was slippery for horses and water had to be ferried on mules from a nearby spring. Ten years later he was still grappling with the boundaries of his estate. He retired in 1843, going home to England to become a member of several scientific societies till he passed away on the first day of December 1866.

Five years later, Sir Andrew Waugh suggested that the great peak should be named after his illustrious predecessor.

Sherpas

Any story on the Nepal Himalayas would be incomplete if mention were not made of the indomitable Sherpas. Once the mountains were opened up, climbers risked life and limb to get to the summit. And were it not for the Sherpas, these peaks would have literally remained the legendary Abode of the Gods.

Dwelling in the very heart of the Himalayas, against the backdrop of the eternal snows in the Solo and Khumbu districts in Eastern Nepal, the Sherpas lead a pastoral existence, tilling their calcinated fields of terraced land. They are stoics, grazing their yaks on tender grass after the snow melts. Never heard to complain, with a ready smile they welcome all those who intrude upon the peaceful tenor of their ways. Maybe it has more to do with their faith—Buddhism—which teaches one to be detached from material things. How else can one explain their fortitude? Officially they made their entry into the orbit of mountaineering in 1907 when Dr A. M. Kellas employed a few lads from Darjeeling on a trip to the Sikkim Himalayas. There has been no looking back since then and the mark of sturdy mountainfolk made its entry into the record books.

Among the first was Sherpa Chettan, nicknamed the Tiger, who in 1924 helped bring Norton down from the North Col of Everest after he was struck with snowblindness. Six years later, on a second expedition to Kangchenjunga he was killed in an avalanche.

Then in 1934 there was Gayley, who made the ultimate choice of staying back on Nanga Parbat with Willy Merkl, rather than abandoning his leader and getting away to safety. Their bodies were found lying together years later and were buried under a granite prominence.

Twenty-eight year old Pasang Kikuli, one of the lucky few to survive a horrible disaster on Nanga Parbat in 1934, paid no heed to his own safety five years later as he climbed K2 with two other Sherpas in a truly brave attempt to rescue Wolfe, a member of an American expedition who lay alone in Camp VII after being sick. On Day One of the rescue attempt, the three climbed from Base Camp to Camp VI—a feat unparalleled in the annals of bravery. Next day the trio reached Camp VII at 24,706 feet. They were never seen again.

Tales of individual acts of heroism abound. Buried by an avalanche during an expedition to Cho-Oyu, Wangdi, buried under the snow, sturggled for three hours before he managed to free himself.

In matters of honour and loyalty, the Sherpas have no equal. By 1954, Pasang Dawa Lama had climbed quite a few peaks already and was with an Austrian expedition to Cho Oyu when a Swiss expedition re-routed their own objective to the same summit. Pasang would have none of this. In pique, he climbed from Marlung at 13,000 feet, near Namche Bazar, to the very summit in three days, reaching 26,867 feet without oxygen!

The number of Sherpas accompanying the early expeditions were usually quite large. Having seen a cavalcade of 350 porters going up the mountains on an Everest expedition, Eric Shipton decided to come back with the minimum possible. In 1934, he had with him Angtharkey, Pasang, Bhutia and Kusang, of whom he was to write later:

'Among the many delights of the Nanda Devi venture was that, for the first time, I was able to treat these people (the Sherpas) as friends rather than hired porters and servants. Sharing with them our food and our tent space, our plans and our problems, we came to know their individual characteristics and to appreciate their delicious humour and their generous comradeship in a way that is quite impossible on a large expedition.'

Facing page: Fire and ice. Climbers warming themselves at a high-altitude campsite.
Following pages 84-85: Mt. Nuptse (7,829 m).

Left: A charming old woman from Bhutan
Right: Kashmiri bakkarwal women with their typical embroidered caps.

A little girl being carried by her big sister (Nepal).

Left: Tamang lady from Nagar Kot
Right: Young Garhwali woman with her large silver earrings and head scarf.

Left: An elder of the Brok-pa tribe of the Da Hanu region of Ladakh, wearing his typical cap decorated with flowers.

Right: The Rani of Zangla. The turquoise-studded head gear (perak) is worn by married women in Ladakh as a sign of wealth.

Ladakh: Childhood habits will surface even if one is training to be a monk!

Left: A monk of the Gelugpa sect of Buddhism at Rumtek monastery, Sikkim.

Right: A young bride from Kinnaur (Himachal Pradesh) with her traditional silver jewellery and head gear.

Sometimes, walking through the mountains of the Himalayas, if you pause a moment to catch your breath besides a boulder, you will wonder why so many flowers insist upon a crevice to thrust their roots into? Take the saxifrage, your a-typical rock-plant. All the members of this vast family can flourish among the rocks— that boulder which looks so solid that no plant can ever hope to get any sustenance from it, yet there it is!

Another lover of the rocky soil is the *oxalis* or wood-sorrel which takes over entire slopes during the monsoon. Its pretty mauve flower, set amidst a cluster of heart-shaped leaflets, is unmistakable. The hill-folk call it the *khatta-mitha*, or the sweet-sour because of the mild acidity of its leaves. Often you'll find people sitting in the sun polishing the brass-base of their *hookahs* with its leaves in autumn. And if some bumbler swallows the poisonous seeds of the *dhatura* by accident, the juice of the plant will always help.

Anothe sorrel, though very different, grows in the hills. Unlike the modest *oxalis*, the sheep sorrel is a tough weed; it grows among rocks, the walls of old houses, and in soils which refuse to support any other plant life. The flowers, which appear in the spring and autumn, are pink and red flakes, rather like confetti. They too are acidic (in fact, sorrel does mean sour), and though sheep sorrel may have been thought fit only for sheep, its near-relative, sorrel-dock, was once eaten along with mutton.

In August watch out for the cobra-lily that steals forth silently across the mushy forest floor. It looks so real that no bird or beast will dare come near it. Look close by, the pale mauve of the *ladies-slipper* hugs the ground. It is tender and vulnerable to even a passing shadow. Tougher is the *ladies-mantle* looking like some piece of crochet.

When the tedium of the drip, drip, drip of the rains is over, it's time to rejoice with the convolvulus' trumpet flowers pronouncing that the sun has finally emerged victorious from its bout with the clouds. The crowning glory of all the wildflowers is the *fein-kamal*, growing just below the snowline. Innumerable tales and legends have woven their way around it. A favourite is the one

BLOOMS

told by grandmothers in the cobbled courtyards of the villages of the Himalayas. Once upon a time, as all stories go, there dwelt a miserable old miser who refused to part with his riches and gems. Even when the king asked him for just a few gems to decorate the dome of a new temple, the miser shook his head and said no.

When his only daughter fell ill in his old age, the miser realized that instead of hiding his gems, he could have given them to someone who could have cured his daughter. He set out to bring them but on the way he fell and died. No one seems to know what happened to his daughter, but one day, from the earth where the gems were believed to be buried sprang the most stunning cluster of flowers, flecked with the colour of the gems that bore them. The *fein-kamal* was born!

Some believe that if you see a praying-mantis atop a *fein-kamal*, it brings the climber good luck. Just like Saint John's Wort or Word—a flower of dazzling sunshine reputed to banish evil. Many legends spring from its spiky leaves. Do you suffer from madness? Drink the red sap oozing from its leaves. Your wound will not heal? Take the juice, put it on the wound and be whole again. Are you bald? Rise early to rub the dew off the petals on the bald pate.

Then there is the blue Himalayan poppy, elusive as ever in the wild. Blue, deeper than the blue you've ever seen. Nature's favourite colour. You can see it in little crannies, encrusted with dew, catching the rays of the rising sun. Its life is brief but beautiful. How well we know that the beauty of flowers is destined to fade, but what goes in flowers is not what one cares for; the beauty lies in the love that never perishes, and year after year, as the seasons melt into each other, new flowers bloom afresh, to be looked at all over again.

In the Himalayas, one can find a hundred varieties of flowers. The rhododendrons bloom in March and light up the forests with their scarlet flashes. In the meadows light blue and yellow anemones flourish while marigolds line the grassy water beds. Potentillas, primroses, primulas and orchids grow in abundance everywhere. The purple saffron flower (which provides the exotic spice) is grown extensively in the Kashmir valley. Flowers are grown not only for their beauty but also for their medicinal and healing powers.

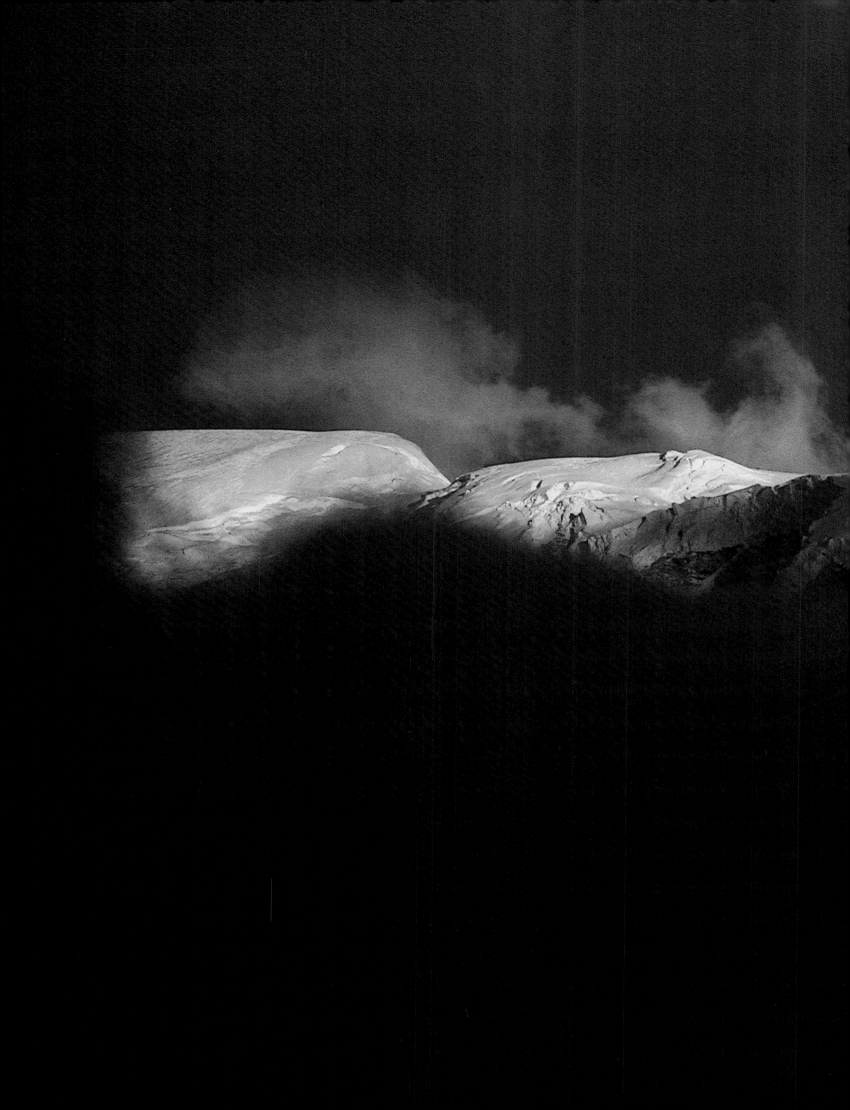

Chapter 5

SIKKIM AND BHUTAN

The Chumbi valley forms the border between Sikkim and Bhutan and the Great Himalayas pass through it. The delights of the Sikkim Himalayas were revealed to the world by Sir Joseph Dalton Hooker, an eminent naturalist and close friend of Charles Darwin. Exploring the area from 1848 to 1850, he discovered twenty-two species of rhododendrons alone. In *Himalayan Journals* he takes the reader by the hand through a landscape covered not just by flowers alone, but people and peaks, scattered all over the region.

His travels took him through the alpine regions, where he spent over six months. He climbed up to the passes bordering Tibet and his wanderings brought him very close to the base of Kanchenjunga. From a spur he looked westwards and wrote: 'There was no continuous snowy chain; the Himalayas seemed suddenly to decline into black, rugged peaks, till in the far north-west it rose again in a white mountain mass of stupendous elevation at 80 miles distance, called by my Nepalese people *Tsungau.*' What he was seeing in the distance was a mountain, the highest in the world—Mount Everest.

Caught in a torrential monsoon downpour, he found his mind, trained to be scientific, musing on the eternal cycles of cosmic unity as seen in the titanic struggles of nature: 'Upon what a gigantic scale does nature operate . . . ! Vapours raised from an ocean whose nearest route is more than four hundred miles distant safely transported without loss of one drop of water to support the rank luxuriance of this far distant region. This and other offices fulfilled, the waste waters are returned by the rivers to the ocean, and again exhaled, exported, recollected and returned.'

Echoing Darwin's 'survival of the fittest', he found that even the innocuous kingdom of the flowers was eternally at war as he wrote: 'Plants in a state of nature are always warring with one another, contending for the monopoly of the soil.' Even subtle changes of climate or soil would only favour one at the cost of the other.

Sikkim beyond Kanchenjunga.

However, the pioneer of mountaineering in Sikkim was a shy, introvert Scotsman, Alexander Mitchell Kellas. Concerned about the effect altitude could have on the human body, he was content to write papers on this theme but of his climbing he has left no record. Kenneth Mason observed: 'Perhaps no climber has enjoyed himself more among the Sikkim Himalayas than Dr Kellas.' He went to the area in 1907, conserving his energies on the Zemu glacier while trying to get to the Nepal Gap and came

means the five treaure houses of the great snows. It is said that once under the five peaks lay the hidden treasures of the Himalayas, guarded by five demons. The younger demons, three in number, were not too happy with the other two elders. They conspired to carry away the most valuable treausre, but this was not so easy, for the secret—which peak held the treasure—was known only to the eldest demon.

In order of seniority, from the eldest to the youngest, the demons were the tiger, the lion

Rumtek monastery, Sikkim, with a statue of the Seated Buddha. Rumtek is the headquarters of the Kagyupa sect of Tibetan (lamaistic) Buddhism.

back several times to explore the region. Selected to accompany the first expedition to the Everest, he was not to make it, as he died quite suddenly of cardiac arrest on the approach through Tibet.

With the Siwaliks no longer there, the Great Himalaya in Sikkim faces the plains to the south. Northwards it is fragmented; broken up by the rivers Arun and the Tamur Kosi to the west and to the east by the many tributaries of the Tista. In the middle rises Kanchenjunga, the third highest peak in the world, approachable from all four sides as the mountains seem to rise towards the peak itself.

The Ghoom Rock in Darjeeling, from where you get the best view of the famous peak, has a very interesting legend connected with how it got there. It is believed that 'Kanchenjunga'

the elephant, the horse and the roc bird. While the last three were conspiring, the demon of Everest got a whiff of the vile plot to rob the Himalayas. He shrugged and an earthquake rocked the mountains and a part of the peak held by the elephant broke and fell. In the dark stormy night, the three demons met and the elephant told his fellow conspirators that the peak he was guarding had broken off the night before and it probably had the treasure they wanted. So they could cart it off and start a new world.

The roc bird lifted the peak, the elephant carried it on his back and the horse simply pushed along. Soon they started squabbling over who was not doing enough and as the three let go, they dropped the rock at the spot where the Ghoom rock now stands in Darjeeling. Of the fabled treasure, no one knows anything, for the rock will not move till the three demons get together again!

Numerous glaciers are strewn all over the mountains of Sikkim, the better-known ones being Janu, Yalung, Talung and Zemu. The easier one to visit is Zemu, while going from Gangtok through Chumthang and Lachen.

Sikkim remains the only state in India which is predominantly Buddhist, where the whirlwind of change has only simplified life for the mountainfolk. In this small state there are over

Chogyal Phuntsang Namgyal, the first ruler of Sikkim, by a Buddhist called Lama Phutsang Lahutsun Champo. The Bhutias, Lepchas and Newars keep the fires of faith burning here.

The picturesque Tashiding Monastery is some 103 kilometres from Gangtok and it has been said that any journey to Sikkim is only half done till the visitor has set his eyes on this special place. Built in 1716 on the hill between Rangit and Ratong rivers, it is like a veritable pot of gold at the end of the rainbow.

Yellow Hat lamas with trumpets at the Rumtek Monastery in Sikkim.

seventy monasteries and a glimpse into these is a journey into the heart of faith. Mahayana Buddhism advocated the all-embracing nature of sympathy, and the emptiness of existence with no other goal than Buddhahood itself. In the 8th century, the faith began to decline in India and spread abroad to China, Japan and Tibet. The lesser school, the Hinayana, remains preserved today in Ceylon, Burma, Cambodia and Thailand.

It was the great guru Padmasambhava who brought the faith to Sikkim and he is remembered in the land as the second incarnate Buddha. Among the many monasteries scattered over the land are: Pemyangtse, Tashidding, Rumtek, Dadarul, Phodang, Ralang, Anchey and Phensang.

The Pemyangtse Monastery sits atop a hillock at a height of some 6,500 feet and is reputed to be 350 years old. It was built during the reign of

Rumtek Monastery is only twenty-five kilometres from Gangtok and echoes of Tibet resound in its delicate architecture. It is the focal point for young novitiates to the faith and is a living monastery.

BHUTAN

Chomolhari rises like an aged sentinel guarding the border at 23,997 feet, to be followed in quick succession by several unnamed peaks ranging in height from 24,720 feet to 23,750 feet.

The highest peak in the Bhutan Himalayas is Kula-Kangri at 24,784 feet and the Great Himalayas run on to enter India in Arunachal Pradesh. Bhutan, the 'Land of the Thunder Dragon', has been all but closed to a handful of foreigners. Seeped in lamaist culture, cut off from the outside world for centuries, Bhutan has just begun to emerge from a self-imposed isolation to a very strictly controlled tourism. The cost of living is high, the highest in the world, as just being in Bhutan, whether walking, climbing or trekking, costs a minimum of $200 per day. This has helped the place to resist declining into a haven for low-budget tourism—the bane of hill-stations in India—or into Kathmandu's hippie trail.

As one crosses the border with India at

A huge thongdrel *(Bhutanese name for* thangka*) tapestry at Paro Tsechu. A thongdrel is a 'banner which brings liberation by sight'.*

mist from which the forest tries, only tries, to peer and succeeds in looming like a ghost, forever baleful. Here, the whole forest seems to be part of another much older world than the tangled woods you leave behind. Down there, in the vernal humidity, the jungle breeds new life continually; vines and creepers struggling with each other to get to the light and in the process covering everything, nay, everything in a mantle of green.

Creepers and lianas drape themselves around

Phuntsholing, the landscape changes rapidly into a fairyland with mist-enveloped streams and waterfalls breaking the silence of dense forests. It is in these first ranges that the monsoon pours its copious waters. And when it rains, it rains all through the night and all next day, and most of the following night. Sometimes the rain falls softly, wrapping the trees in mist so that they stand ghostly and forlorn, old and dreary, covered with ferns and moss that drip so woefully. Sometimes the rain falls heavily, drowning the murmur of the rivulets that make their tortured way among the trees, fighting and foaming over the rounded rocks and balding boulders. Often it comes with the roll of drums, thundering through the skies, booming in the mountains, while the forests seem to sob with rain.

Your footsteps are muted in the shimmering

the trees like silken veils, as if in a futile attempt to hide the denizens of the green. Yet in the forests higher up, near the crest of the mountains, silence reigns as if nothing had changed since it all began. Bereft of rain, the mist moves in hushed tones in deference to the ageless forest. This knowlege of age is accentuated by the feeling that this is no ordinary forest—it feeds upon its dead, the decaying trees, dead leaves, rotting moss and mouldering fern which gives the old trees enough to feed upon.

And the rocks underfoot are no ordinary rocks either. They hark back to the Sea of Tethys, when fifty million years ago, Atlas shrugged—and the mountains were born. Now covered with mosses, ferns and lichens, they lie humped in silence for another dawn.

When the sun appears, the hillsides are covered with crimson-red masses of rhododendrons and the heady whiff of magnolias scents the air, their blossoms lighting up the gloomy forests. Even the common oak trees are almost unrecognizable, covered and plumed with ferns, of a shape you're not going to find elsewhere.

Crossing the barrier of the forests, you descend to the main valley, lush and fertile,

the entire facade of the Lhakhang and is said to be so sacred that wars have been waged for its possession.

A Tsechu is a festival to commemorate one of the miracles wrought by the great Guru Padmasambhava or Rimpoche, who is said to have brought the faith here. The Sacred Thangka, viewed by thousands of devotees, is supposed to depict the great guru in his eight manifestations and is thus a 'thongdrel', considered esoterically so powerful that it

Lamas folding a big thongdrel *which is exhibited for a few hours on one day during the Paro Tsechu festival.*

where naturally, the bulk of the population dwells. Over twenty thousand people live in Thimpu, the present-day capital of Bhutan. Thimpu has been the seat of power since 1960, when King Jingme Dorje Wangchuk converted the Thashi Cho Dzong monastery into a royal palace, but the main monastery is still the second largest place of worship in the land. The largest and by far the most magnificent is the Paro Monastery, home to the hall of the Thousand Buddhas and much more. If you take a walk, you'll understand why the icy pyramid of Chomolhari has been called one of the most beautiful peaks in the Himalayas.

For the tourist, the highlight of festivals in Bhutan is the five-day Paro Tsechu. On the last day, a 400-year-old *thangka*, a tantric Buddhist scroll, is unfurled. It is so huge, it covers almost

can release an ordinary mortal from the endless cycles of reincarnation forever.

For the Bhutanese, the Paro Tsechu is also a social occasion on which old acquaintances are renewed, new friendships forged and fresh ties made. For five days, it is holiday time and trysts are made and unmade as young and old, the beautiful and the ugly, the weak and the strong flock to see the famed dances of Bhutan. After the merry-making, the festivities come to an end, the *thongdrel* is rolled up and put away in the monastery, to be unfurled at the next Tsechu.

A veil falls over Bhutan again and the world of the Thunder Dragon covers itself, once more, in a splendour of isolation.

Following page 96: *Ladakhi children muffled up against the cold.*